Smocking
with a
Difference

16 refreshingly different, new and stylish 'Jigsaw' smocking designs

Jan McNess

Aird Books

MELBOURNE

Aird Books Pty Ltd
PO Box 122
Flemington, Vic. 3031
Australia

First published by Aird Books in 1994

National Library of Australia
Cataloguing-in-publication data

McNess, Jan, 1941-.
  Smocking with a difference.

  ISBN 0 947214 39 9.

  1. Smocking. I. Title.

746.44

Cover design by Helen Semmler
Text design by Pauline McClenahan, Captured Concepts
Photography by John Brennan and David Gorrie
Stitch diagrams by Yang Qin Lin, stitch illustrations by
  Bronwyn Halls
Printed by Impact Printing, Melbourne, Australia

Contents

In Memory of Jeremy

The laughter in our days
The superman of our dreams
The inspiration for 'the Shirt'

Introduction

Smocking is surely one of the most satisfying of all crafts. It possesses all the elements one normally hopes to find in a craft. It is practical, it is satisfying, it is creative and, the added bonus, there is a market for it.

Traditional smocking has certainly stood the test of time. The earliest known piece, which was found in marsh land in Denmark, almost perfectly preserved, has been carbon dated to 1175 BC. (It makes you feel there's something to be said for mud packs, if not complete mud baths, after all!)

There have been many variations on the main theme over time, but its primary function has never changed: to control gathering in a garment and to make that garment fit the human form more closely.

Forms of smocking have appeared in many different cultures around the world during this time, often with slight regional differences. Sometimes the elasticity, so prized in English smocking, is completely absent and the emphasis is more on intricate stitching forming geometric design. At other times, the emphasis is on elasticity and more simple forms of embroidery.

In recent times, it has been associated mainly with children's clothing, although that was not always the case. Several centuries ago it reached a great high point in its history when the 'smock' became the main form of dress for rural workers, particularly men and children in Britain. This came about because of its functional properties as it allowed freedom of movement not so easily achieved in the more closely fitting garments of the day.

These early smocks had small amounts of smocking on the chest, across the back of the shoulders and at the tops of the sleeves – in fact, in all the places where some 'give' in the garment was needed. Normally, the smock was made by the wife and she used her embroidery skills to smock not only where it was necessary but also to embroider small symbols down either side of the front opening to denote her husband's type of work. Perhaps a sheaf of wheat would signify a farmer, a sheep a shepherd, an axe a woodcutter, and so on. It would be possible to tell the occupation of a person at a glance.

It was at this stage that Feather Stitch became an accepted companion stitch to smocking, once again for practical rather than decorative purposes. Of course, all work was done by hand and, to reinforce seams, Feather Stitch was used with one side of the stitch on the right-hand side of the seam and the other side of the stitch on the left of the join. What was achieved was a mix of functional and decorative stitching.

As times changed, and with mechanisation becoming a normal part of life, loose fitting clothing was no longer practical, in many cases very dangerous, so smocking transferred almost entirely to the decoration of women's and children's clothing.

The functional property of smocking recognised so long ago, is still the reason for its continuing popularity, although now its decorative potential is of equal importance. The appearance of a fabric can be enhanced by smocking which at the same time increases the usefulness and fit of a garment.

In the last 10-15 years there has been another major factor affecting the popularity of smocking. It has, in fact, been largely responsible for a great resurgence in this craft: the development and gradual perfecting of the pleater machine. In contemporary post-industrial societies many people feel they do not have the time to spend in preparing (gathering) fabric for smocking and, therefore, this machine has proved a great boon.

It is the potential for decoration which drew me originally, and which still draws me to smocking. However, after twenty years or more of traditional smocking, the restrictions of tradition were beginning to tell and I needed something more creative. 'Jigsaw' smocking, or interpretive smocking, is the answer for me.

Just as in traditional smocking, there are many more applications for 'Jigsaw' smocking than just small girls' dresses, although I must admit that this is still my favourite form of expression. However, in this book I would like to introduce you to some of the other applications I have found.

It is ideal for both adult and children's clothes, and just as good for males as for females. It is perfect for linking one piece of clothing with another, e.g. a shirt with a skirt or trousers; a shirt with a particular tie; or a shirt, a dress or trousers with a hat. In fact, the options are so many and varied that it is only lack of imagination which can hold this craft back.

For people interested in the craft but not in clothing: once again, let your imagination run wild! A wonderful wall hanging to set off a particular colour scheme, beautiful napkin rings to enhance a table setting, small gifts such as a miniature sampler made into a lavender bag or potpourri sachet. The scope is wide, the opportunities are great.

Stitch Diagrams

The smocking stitches are represented in the diagrams of the projects in the following way:

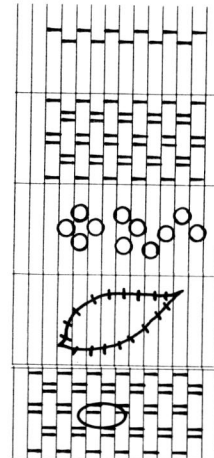

Cables

Stacked Cables

French Knots

Outline Stitch

Bullion Stitch

1

'Jigsaw' Smocking

Most crafts began with the germ of an idea, based on necessity. Then, the original, simple form becomes more complex as the craft develops. Each new direction opens up possibilities for further ideas and creativity. Whenever another person takes up a craft, or as exponents of that particular craft explore further directions, there is always the chance something new will emerge. 'Jigsaw' smocking is such a development. The Jigsaw method is a complete process in which all the elements of colour, fabric pattern and stitches combine to develop and determine an overall design. It offers great opportunities for original work, interpreting fabric patterns into smocking designs. A logical 'next' step in this sequence is either to design your own fabrics or to commission fabrics to your own design and to then interpret these fabrics with Jigsaw smocking.

This style of smocking works successfully because the functional aspect of smocking is recognised and provided by the rows of smocking which must be worked across the back of each piece of work. This stitching holds the pleats in place and gives the work its elasticity, both essential aspects of the smocking technique. The most effective stitch to use for this 'backsmocking' in Jigsaw smocking is Cable. This is best worked first, before starting on the front of the decorative panel, as it becomes more difficult if you leave it till last. This stitch is least intrusive on the front of the panel, especially if care is taken to pick up only the smallest amount of each pleat. Once the purely

functional necessities have been met, the front of the work presents itself to you, just as a new canvas does to the artist!

Most designs are started in the centre of the panel as this allows the greatest flexibility in design, and gives the greatest opportunity to balance the colour scheme. Once a shape has been worked to cover the centre section of the panel, the design is gradually built by working in diagonally opposite directions radiating out from this central point. As you work, there is ample opportunity for checking colour and design balance regularly, to ensure a pleasing effect.

However, some designs cannot be started from the centre pleat, e.g. the Playsuit, the Child's Denim Shirt Pocket and the Dungaree's Pocket. It will be quickly obvious that these designs necessarily start on the left-hand side and are worked straight across to the right.

Many of the projects in this book can be copied, but others give great scope for creativity if you wish to try your hand at design. The diagrams show central sections of many of the designs and it is possible either to follow the photographed articles or to branch out on your own having first built a base on which to work.

Pockets are ideal projects when starting out on Jigsaw smocking. Each is small enough not to become a 'life-long' project, yet big enough to test yourself. As each pocket is complete in itself, it is easy to swap them between garments, so a favourite pocket has its useful life extended dramatically.

A further adventure to take in Jigsaw smocking is shown in the Denim Dungarees (pages 23 and 28), the Child's Denim Shirt (pages 26 and 29), and the Playsuit (pages 27 and 32).

For these projects it is not necessary to back-smock as the designs are both decorative and functional. This is because each pleat is joined to its immediate neighbour on either side, thus holding all pleats in place and allowing elasticity. If you choose to try this variation, it is preferable to use a reasonably heavy fabric, e.g. chambray, some pure cottons, Homespun, some woollen fabrics, etc. It is necessary to keep the stitching very even so that it is possible to trace each row of stitching from one side of the smocked panel to the other, although each different coloured shape is completed before moving onto the next. I always use three strands of embroidery floss for this type of smocking.

Jigsaw smocking opens up new avenues as it offers a more sophisticated aspect to this form of embroidery. Tapestry and Cross Stitch designs readily adapt to Jigsaw designs. Knitting designs can also be used as ideas on which to build. However, its greatest advantage is its creativity and the opportunity to make each item or garment a 'one-off'.

Colour in jigsaw smocking

Though personal opinions differ vastly on colour – particularly on the colours which suit one person but not another – no-one would ever deny the power of its effect on us and our surroundings.

We associate pink/apricot/red with warmth and we see these colours as warm and welcoming. Green and blue are seen as 'cool' colours, often used when we wish to create a calm, soothing environment. Yellow is associated with joy and is linked with spring and new life. White denotes purity and innocence and black is seen as 'smart' and is also associated with sadness and mourning.

Thus, colour reflects and creates moods and emotions and many well-known sayings in our culture directly relate to colour – e.g. 'seeing red', 'feeling blue', 'looking green', 'in a black mood', 'a grey outlook'. We all understand immediately what is meant by such statements.

Colour inspires our song writers and poets to rise to great lyrical and musical heights. We sing with gusto of 'Lavender Blue', 'Yellow Submarine',

'Greensleeves', 'Cherry Ripe', 'Yellow Rose of Texas', and are touched by poetry such as 'The Primrose', 'To Violets', 'To Daffodils', 'Pied Beauty' – all delighting in the colour of nature and our surroundings.

Australians are in a unique position to take advantage of the multicultural diversity in the Australian population, each culture bringing new and exciting aspects to the developing Australian culture. We have opportunities, not available in most other countries, to foster the great diversity of our people and to use and build on the 'colour' this gives to our culture.

To the rest of the world we are a young, still emerging country. We should always strive to forge our own way in every possible field, including the arts and crafts. We are continually gaining more recognition in these areas and must foster this at every level.

Colour is where we differ from so much of the rest of the world. From our clear blue skies to the stark golden orange of the sun, the red interior, the turquoise-green ocean surrounding our land, and the grey-green of our Eucalypt landscape – we are different.

Let us use this difference. Let us enjoy and promote the starkness and brashness of colour produced in our particular conditions. Let us use it in our art and crafts, making it an instantly recognisable feature of Australian culture.

Jigsaw smocking is an opportunity to use colour as a statement – to recognise its power to please the eye and to affect our mood and feelings. Colour in clothing can lift our spirits, can turn a 'grey' day into a bright one. Splashes of colour in a room can highlight and 'lift' an otherwise ordinary aspect. Recognise and use the power of colour in everyday life and be aware that the changes it makes are much deeper than mere cosmetic alteration.

There are many ways to experiment with colour but, for me, the most successful way to learn to use colour is by observation. Really look at nature, really observe a garden of mixed flowers, really see the colour. See ways to combine colours so that one sets off another. Look at fabrics, observe their colour schemes, and choose the ones that please you. Gaze at racks of stranded cottons or tapestry wools, all set out in graduating shades. Buy yourself 24 textas and experiment with colour combinations. Notice how large amounts of one colour, (perhaps purple) may have a dulling effect on a design. Lessen the amount of purple and increase one of the other colours. Note the change this makes. Learn that you can use the colours you like, though sometimes you may need to decrease amounts of one colour and add more of another to achieve the effect you have in mind. Remember that small touches of black and/or white may completely 'lift' any design.

Don't be afraid to experiment with colour. Children are normally very attracted to bright, clear colours. Notice their favourites and work them into colour schemes – encourage children to experiment and appreciate colour in all its diversity. Allow colour to brighten your life and the lives of those around you.

Stranded cotton is used unless otherwise indicated, and the number of strands is given for each project.

For further information on 'Jigsaw' smocking, see Jan McNess' *Smocking with Colour*.

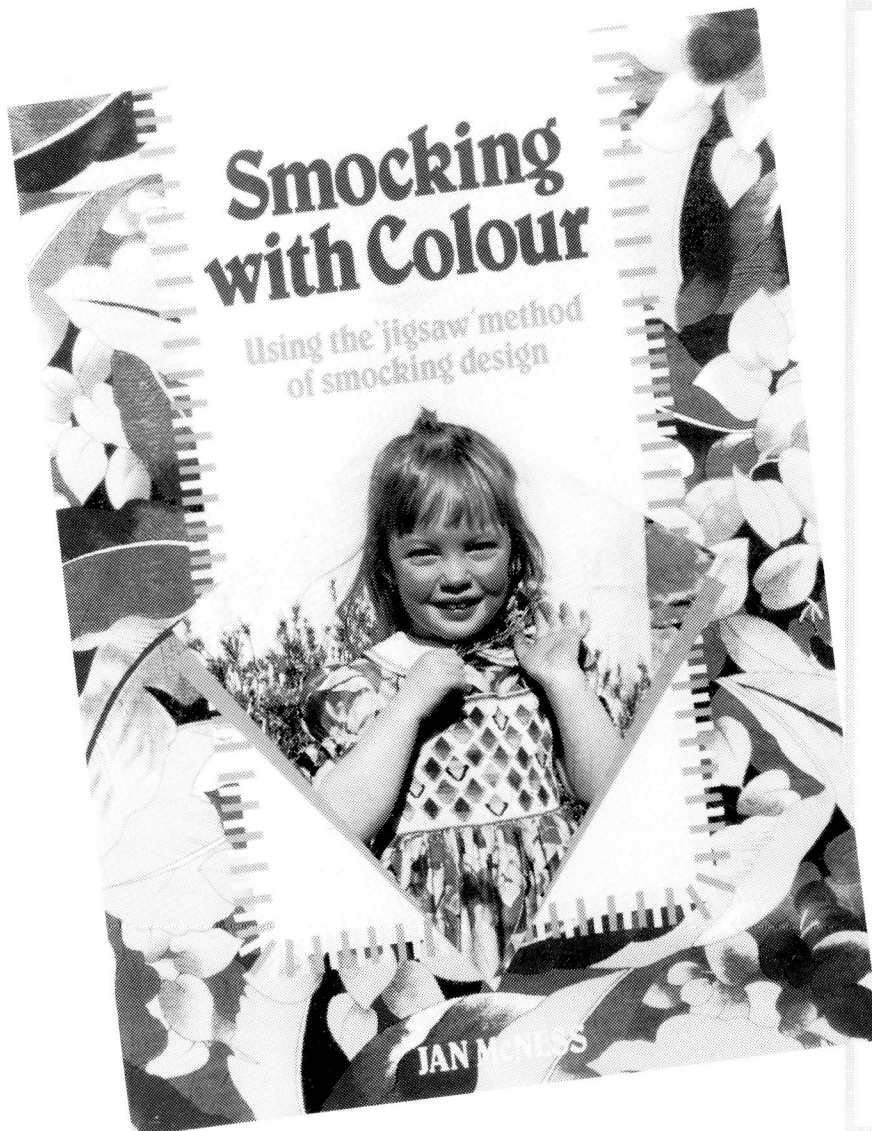

In *Smocking with Colour*,
Jan McNess
gives the traditional
craft of smocking
a brand new look:

'Suddenly I could see ways of turning a wide range of colourful fabrics into inspiring and exciting clothes. Drawing on the boldness of colour and boldness of shape of existing fabric patterns, my Jigsaw method enabled me to develop new smocking designs of great appeal.'

Smocking with Colour tells you how – with diagrams of stitches and designs – you can make your own original and stylish clothes, using Jan McNess's innovative Jigsaw method of smocking.

Large paperback, 60 pages
(12 full-colour pages)
ISBN 0 947214 20 8

2

The Shirt

Shirts for the avant-garde male

The introduction of more colour into men's clothing has really played into the hands of the imaginative craftsperson. There are wonderful ties available at all men's wear shops to suit every taste. Ties can be a great source of inspiration for the jigsaw smocker. However, if this is not inspiration enough, then make your own ties from fabrics of your choice, or decorate them with fabric paints or embroidery. Try using silk fabric and paint your own designs, then enhance the result with a smocked pocket. (Tie patterns are available commercially.)

To buy or not to buy a shirt – that is the question! If you decide to buy a ready-made shirt to match the tie of your choice, you must take into account that you may not be able to find a matching fabric for smocking the pocket. It will be necessary to remove the existing pocket(s) and replace them with a smocked one. Whether the shirt of your choice has one or two pockets will obviously determine the amount of decorative smocking you will have to undertake. Two complete pockets may be too much – perhaps a band on the top of each pocket would be better (see pages 14 and 17). If you are not attempting to match a tie then the design and colour scheme are entirely up to you.

Perhaps you have decided to make your own shirt so that you can choose your fabric. There are many excellent commercial patterns available: choose your favourite and cut out the shirt. You will require an extra 20 cm in length for each pocket.

I prefer to smock the pocket first, then make it up, and then attach it to the shirt front before making up the shirt. Correct placement of the pocket is easiest at that stage. However, it is quite possible to change the order if you wish.

The various decisions you still have to make are:
- how much of the pocket you wish to smock (a band at the top, or the whole pocket);
- the types of thread you will use (ordinary embroidery floss like DMC, Anchor or Semco, or silk thread to match a particular tie); and
- how many strands of thread you would like to use (governed by how bold or delicate you wish the design to be).

Maybe a casual shirt would appeal more to you – after all, hot summer days are not always conducive to wearing ties. Here again, the ideas are many and varied. You have no restrictions on the design and colours you can use because you are not working to a tie design. To link the pocket in with the finished effect, perhaps rows of feather-stitching on the collar to match the colours used on the pocket would complete the picture. Feather-stitching on the cuffs of the sleeves is another alternative.

A fun idea you may like to try is a 'Christmas Shirt' decorated with sparkling Christmas trees. The decorations can be made with tiny French Knots using metallic threads or tiny seed beads. This shirt can be a great piece during the festivities leading up to Christmas and, of course, for the great day itself! You can go further still and decorate the collar with feather-stitching in Christmas colours.

If a 'one-day-a-year' shirt is not your idea of practicality, maybe you need to make two pockets. The second pocket could use a more general theme and then, once Christmas is safely over, this could replace the original pocket which would be put away for next year.

This idea is also great for children's clothing as it is suitable for boys or girls, either as a pocket on shirts or jeans or as a dress or dungarees front. Give the whole family the festive touch – then let the joy of Christmas continue for the whole summer until the garment is worn out, or suggest each family member starts his or her own family heirloom or passes the garment on to a special (smaller) friend or family member.

for an original, wearable artwork for children.

When a lot of effort and thought has gone into designing a pocket, it is great to be able to transfer this to another piece of clothing as the child outgrows the garment. The thought of a child outgrowing a special garment often deters people from putting 'too much' work into a piece of clothing. Denim has been a major clothing fabric for many years now and seems set to stay around for some time to come. Perhaps this is the way to go in children's clothing. Soft denims are ideally suited to the boldness of 'Jigsaw' smocking and lend themselves to strong colours as well as pale ones. There are a number of ideas in this book for using denim and, of course, you will come up with many others.

Shirts for the fashionable, chic female

The shirt will always be an essential part of any wardrobe, and the jigsaw smocked shirt offers the opportunity to own an exclusive piece of clothing! It can look wonderfully elegant or comfortably casual and is guaranteed always to be a conversation piece.

If the shirt is to match an outfit, (i.e. a skirt, a tie, trousers or shorts), then this will necessarily govern colour schemes. Again, you will have to decide whether to buy a ready-made shirt, remove the pocket(s) and replace them with smocked pockets or to make the entire shirt yourself, in which case there are no problems matching fabrics, etc. One little hint (which can come in handy if you have had trouble matching the pocket fabric to the shirt fabric and are afraid that this may show) is to bind the pocket with the contrast fabric of the skirt, shorts, etc. This will divert attention from any slight colour difference.

If you do not wish to smock a pocket for the shirt, you could consider smocking the cuffs. For further instructions, see the diagram and instructions on page 15.

Other variations are to smock the collar and either front yokes or back yoke of the shirt.

Shirts for the 'Jigsaw' kid

As for adults, shirts almost always form part of a child's wardrobe. Again, there is the opportunity

Construction of the pocket

There are general instructions for making a smocked pocket which can be adapted to suit any garment, e.g. the shirt pocket, the dungaree pocket, or the jeans pocket.

The amount of fabric required for a pocket is determined by the size of the pocket. Generally, for an adult's shirt, approximately 20 cm deep and 80 cm wide is sufficient. However, if the fabric is particularly fine (voile, etc), it may be necessary to put more fabric into the width of the smocked piece. For a child's pocket approximately 12 cm deep and 55 cm wide is needed.

Measure the depth of the smocking you would like to have on the pocket, remembering that a band at the top of the pocket gives a tailored finish to the garment. Gather sufficient rows for the depth you require.

Complete the smocking, including the back-smocking, following the instructions for a particular project.

Using either a commercial pocket pattern or the original shirt pocket itself as a pattern, cut out one pocket from an iron-on fabric. I prefer to use iron-on Korlene/Korbond rather than the more popular Vilene, as I find it performs better over a period of time. I also prefer to use a pocket pattern which has a rounded bottom as this is easier to handle when applying bias binding to complete the pocket.

centre pleat

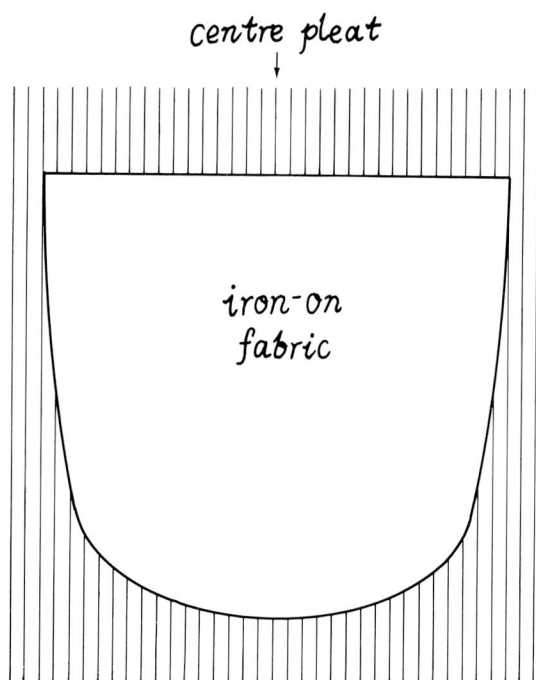

iron-on fabric

Carefully centre the iron-on pocket over the back of the smocked panel and gently press into place.

centre pleat

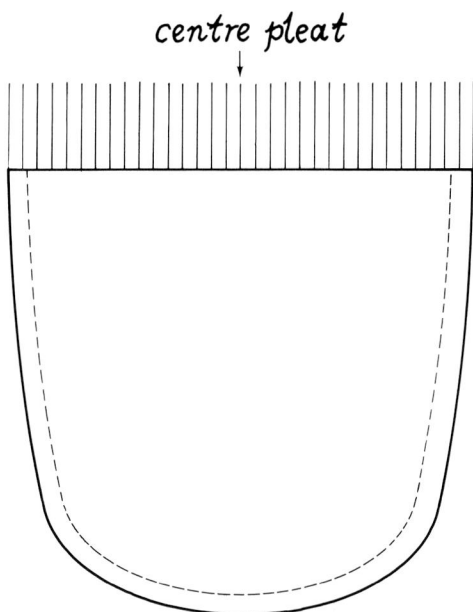

From the back of the pocket, machine-stitch around the pocket, as close to the edge of the iron-on fabric as possible.

Trim away excess smocking that is no longer required.

Pocket Band:

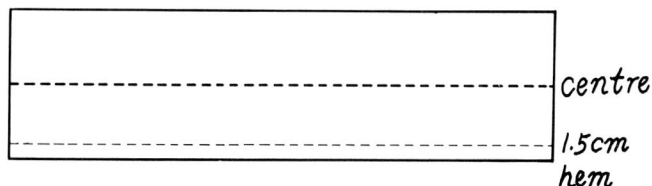

centre

1.5cm hem

- Cut 1 band from the shirt fabric, 9 cm deep by the width of the pocket.
- Cut 1 band from the iron-on fabric, with the same dimensions.
- Apply the iron-on fabric to the band.
- Turn under 1.5 cm hem on one long edge of the band, and press.
- Attach the opposite long edge of the band to the top of the pocket, right sides together, and machine-stitch close to the smocking.
- Fold the band in half and slip-stitch the pressed edge to the back of the pocket.

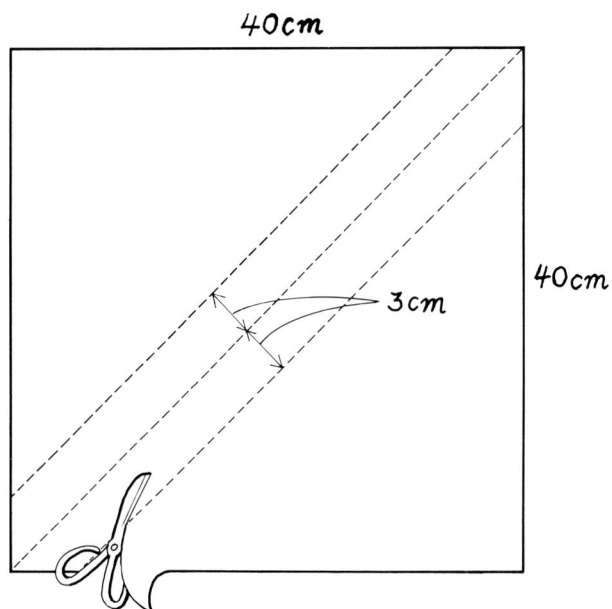

40cm

40cm

3cm

- Using a bias strip of shirt fabric or matching bias-binding, stitch this round the edge of the pocket, right sides together.
- Fold the binding over the edge of the pocket and slip-stitch to the back of the pocket.
- Press gently on the wrong side.

This completed pocket can now be attached to the garment, either by hand or by machine.

Christmas pocket

This shirt is hand-made of poly/cotton fabric, using Simplicity Pattern No. 7330. The project was inspired by the particularly eye-catching tie, and the shirt's base colour too was chosen to offset the tie.

This shirt is just as successful when worn casually without the tie, so it is particularly versatile.

I felt that the tie was so colourful that two full smocked pockets may have detracted from it, so I settled for smocked bands on the pockets instead.

Materials

For each pocket band the fabric required is a piece of 6 cm depth x 80 cm width of the same fabric as the shirt.

Pleating

Pleat 8 half-space rows, centred along fabric strips, leaving two pleats unsmocked at each end.

Smocking

Using 2 strands of embroidery floss, similar in shade to the shirt fabric, back-smock in Cable each row of gathering. Turn to the front and complete the design as shown in the diagram below and the photograph on page 17.

Colours

Use 2 strands of embroidery floss throughout, in the following colours: red, orange, yellow, turquoise, pale turquoise, and white.

To make up

Gently steam smocked bands to fit pocket tops and back with iron-on interfacing. Trim away excess fabric.

Cut 4 bias strips (2 for each pocket) to the same width as the pocket top.

With the right sides together, bind the top and bottom of each smocked band, fold to back and slip stitch in place. Attach the completed bands to the tops of the pockets.

Follow the general instructions in 'Construction of the Pocket' for applying binding to the edges of the pockets, then attach both pockets to the shirt fronts.

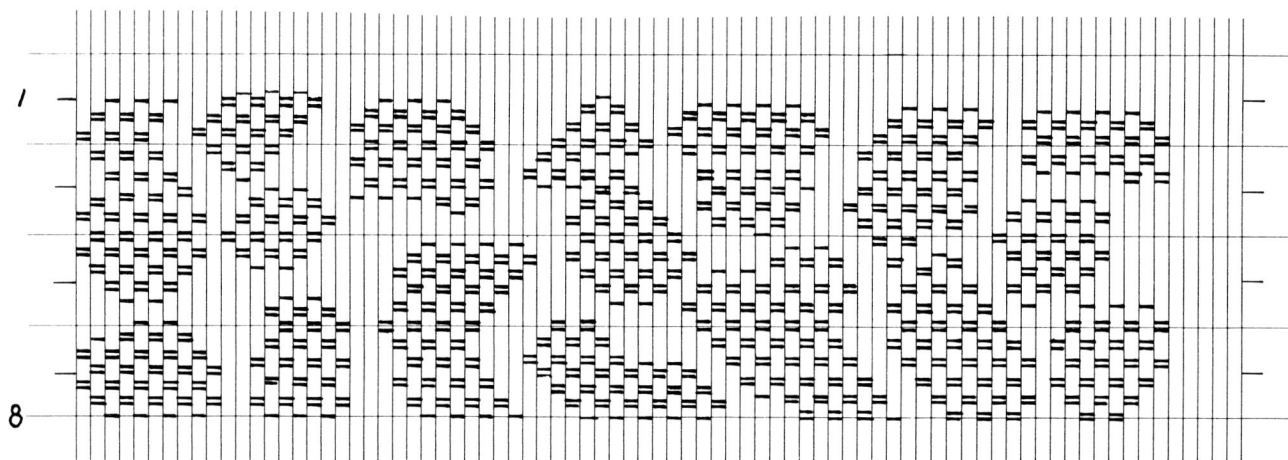

This shirt is an attractive addition to anyone's wardrobe. Any design would be suitable for the smocked cuffs so these could be matched to a favourite skirt or pair of trousers. (Simplicity Pattern No. 7330 using a poly-cotton fabric.)

As the cuffs are fairly bulky, I do not overlap at the opening. Instead, it is better to allow the cuffs just to meet and then to fasten them with buttons and loops.

Materials
For each cuff you need:
- A piece of material 10 cm deep by 105-115 cm wide, depending on the wrist size.
- Iron-on interfacing.
- Bias strips cut from the fabric to bind the cuffs.

Pleating
Pleat 10 rows, including the top and bottom holding rows, and leave 2 pleats unsmocked at each end.

Smocking
Back-smock each gathering row (except for the holding rows) on the back of the work, then turn to the front and follow the diagram below.

Start from the centre pleat on Row 9 for this design and, for the use of colour, see the photograph on page 20.

The design consists of inverted Stacked Cable Pyramids, beginning with one stitch and building up to 7 stitches.

Colours
Use 2 strands of embroidery floss throughout, in the following colours: navy blue, royal blue, mid blue, pale blue, mid green, and pale green.

To make up
Using a cuff pattern piece (as the cuff is going to meet rather than overlap, it must be shortened), cut two from the fabric and two from the iron-on interfacing.

Gently apply interfacing to the back of the cuffs.

Turn up a 1.5 cm hem on one long side of the cuff lining and press. With the right sides together, stitch the lining to interfaced smocking along the short edges, keeping the stitching against the first smocking pleat. Turn to the right side.

Use a bias strip cut to the same length as the cuff, plus seam allowances, and apply this binding to the outside edge of the cuff, right sides together. Turn to the wrong side and hand or machine-stitch the binding in place.

Attach the cuff to the prepared sleeve, right sides together, and complete it by turning it inside out and hand-stitching the pressed edge of the cuff over the trimmed seam.

Complete the other cuff to match, then finish them by making the loops and sewing on the buttons on each cuff.

To finish off, the colours introduced in the cuffs can be echoed in the collar and on the pocket band. I used 1 strand of each colour for this Feather-stitching, so the result would not be too heavy.

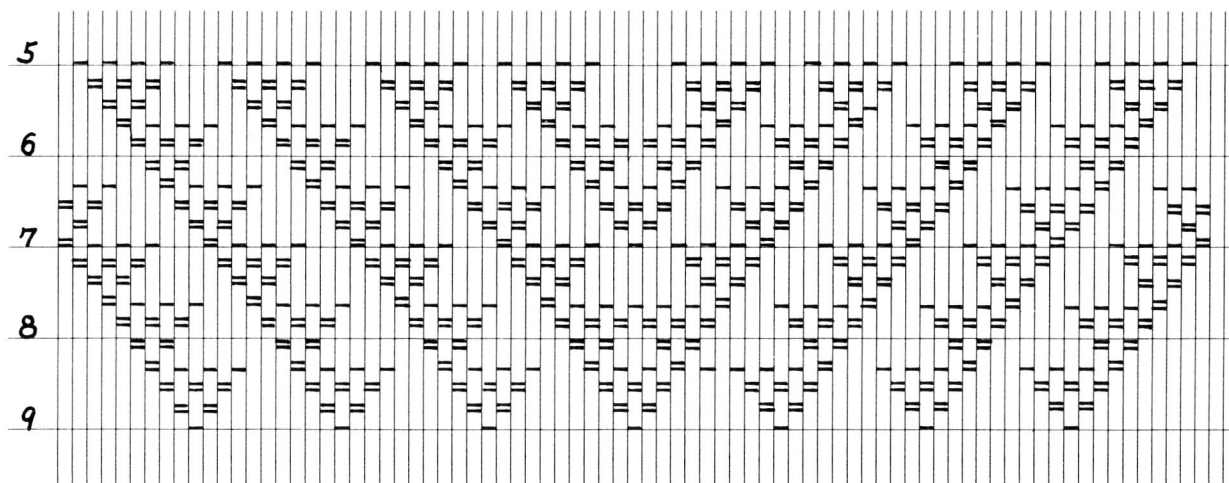

This is a ready-made shirt and the pocket is inspired entirely by the tie. I was attracted to the colours in the tie and to the suggestion of movement which the angular lines appeared to give, as I felt they would translate to smocking design quite easily. The freedom of the design also appealed to me.

Materials

A piece of chambray fabric or another fabric of similar weight, like Homespun, pure cotton or winter cotton of 14 cm deep by 75 cm wide.
Note that this is a coarse fabric, so less is required for the width. If your fabric is finer, a greater width may be required.

Pleating

Pleat 13 rows, including top and bottom holding rows and leave 2 pleats unsmocked at each end.

Smocking

Using two strands of embroidery floss of the same shade as the shirt fabric, back-smock each row of gathering, except for the holding rows.

Turn to the front and complete the pocket, following the diagram below (which only shows the middle section of the pocket) and the photograph on page 21

Colours

Use 3 strands of embroidery floss throughout on this coarser fabric, in the following colours: three shades of purple, deep turquoise, deep olive green, and pale olive green.

To make up

Follow the general instructions for 'Construction of the Pocket' (page 11), then attach it to the shirt in place of the original pocket.

This project is good for the thrifty craftsperson: both the shirt and the tie were purchased at Target.

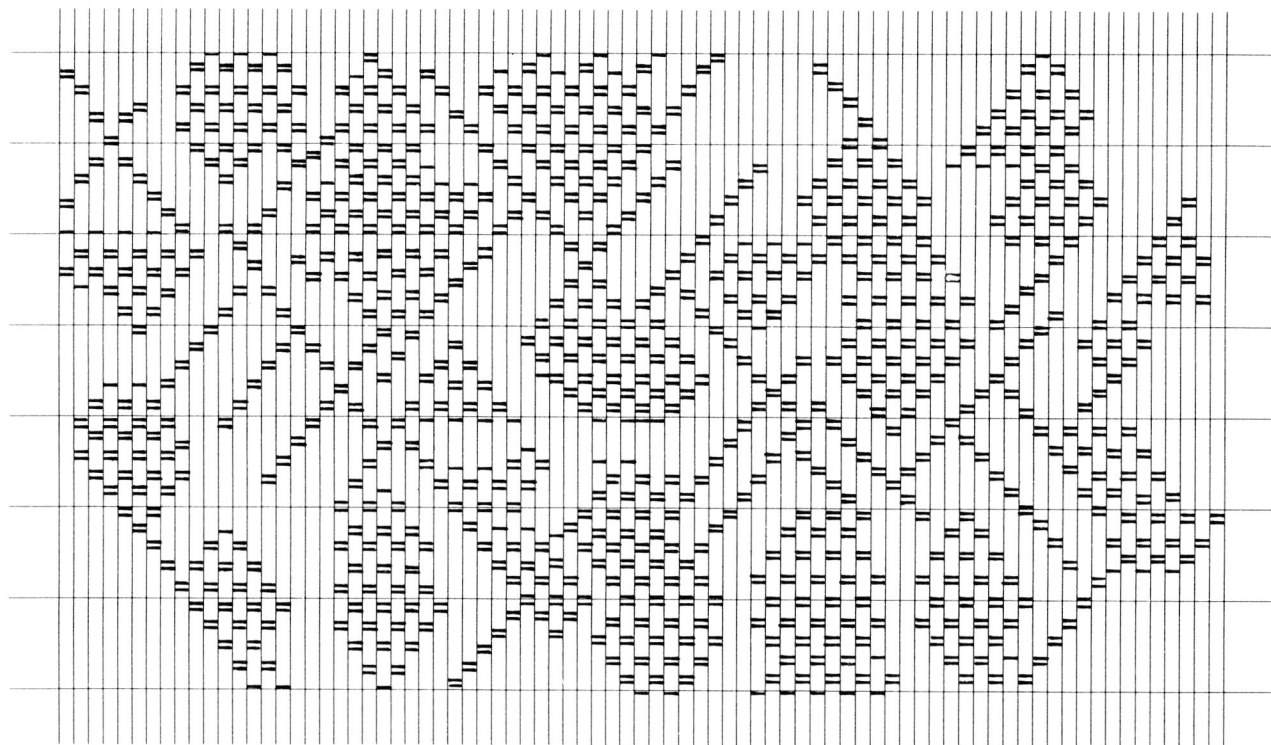

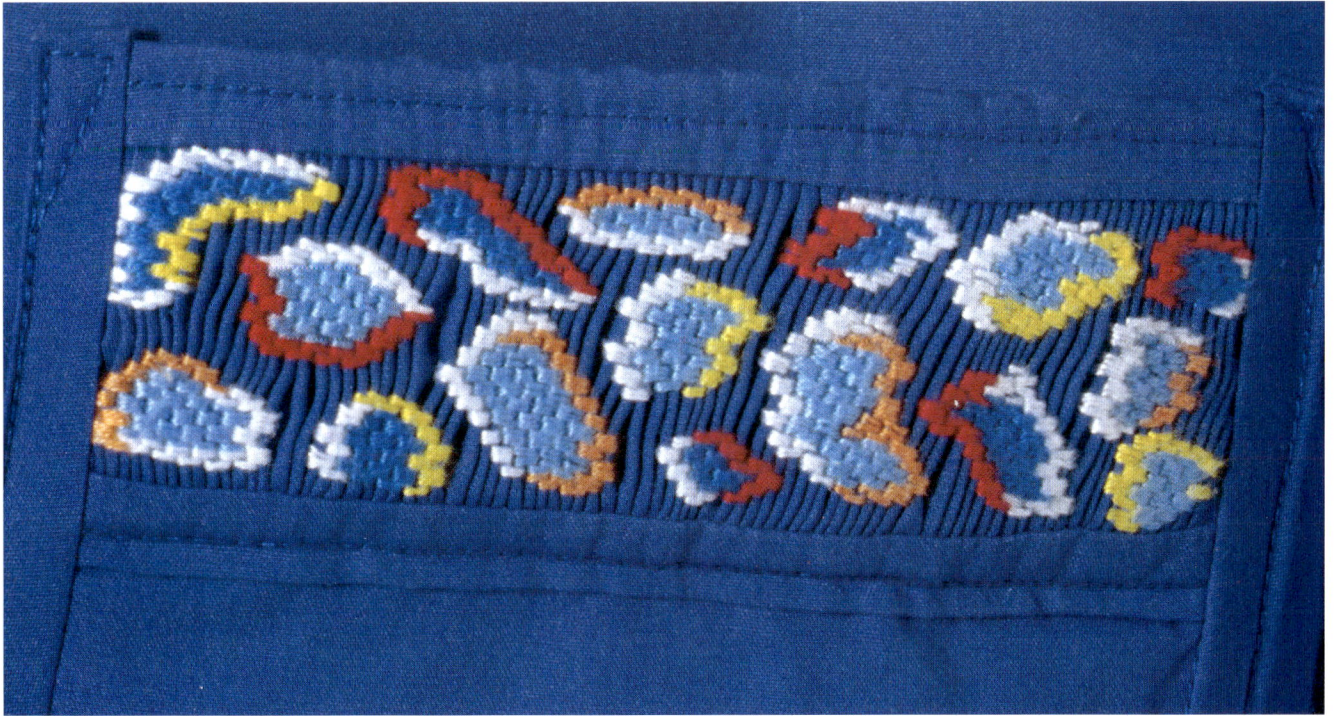

Mid-blue Shirt

I had watched, with some fascination, a fabric-painting class at work, and decided that I would like to try this too.

My project was small. I bought a plain black tie and, using six 'Scribbles Fashion Writer' paints, I painted a simple but effective design. The finished effect was successful. It was then a relatively simple task to mimic this design in smocking for a pocket, which replaced the original on a ready-made shirt.

Materials
- A piece of poly-cotton fabric of 16 cm deep by 90 cm wide. This is a larger than usual pocket, but I had to keep to this size to cover the area of the original pocket.
- Iron-on interfacing.
- Bias strips cut from the fabric to bind the pocket.

Pleating
Pleat 15 rows, including the top and bottom holding rows, and leave 2 pleats unsmocked at each end.

Smocking
Back-smock 13 rows of gathering, not including the holding rows, using 2 strands of matching embroidery floss.

Turn to front and complete the design, following the diagram below (which only shows the middle section of the pocket) and the photograph on page 24.

Colours
Use 2 strands of embroidery floss throughout for this design, in the following colours: dark brown, mid brown, pale brown, tan, fawn, dark grey, light grey.

To make up
Follow the general instructions for 'Construction of the Pocket' (page 11), then attach it to the shirt in place of the original pocket.

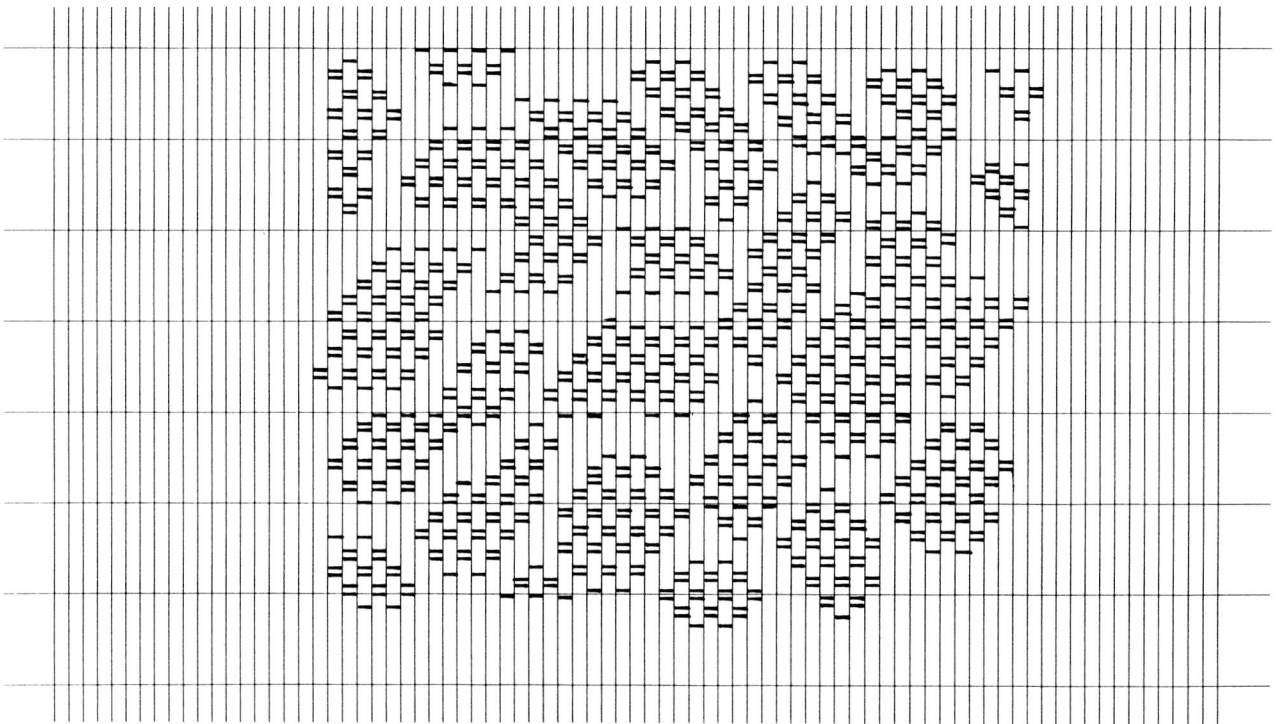

This is a hand-made casual shirt (Simplicity Pattern No. 7330), made to be worn open at the neck. The collar is heavily Feather-stitched to highlight the smocking on the pocket, and the navy buttons echo the colour scheme.

Materials

Just for the pocket you need:

- A 14 cm deep by 75 cm wide piece of Homespun or similar weight fabric.
- A 15-cm piece of iron-on Interfacing
- A 15-cm piece of bias binding or fabric cut on the bias
- A 40-cm piece of bias binding or fabric cut on the bias

Pleating

Pleat 14 rows, including the top and bottom holding rows, and leave 2 pleats unsmocked at each end.

Smocking

Back-smock the entire pocket area with a row of Cable on each row of gathering.

The design is made up of Outline Stitch forming eye-like shapes. I turned my work upside down to smock the under sections of the shapes to achieve continuously flowing lines. Each shape is then filled in, sometimes with Outline Stitch repeated a number of times, sometimes with Stacked Cable shapes, and sometimes with French Knots.

To fill some of the gaps between the eye shapes, I have worked Double Flowerettes.

Photographs of the collar and pocket of the white shirt are shown on page 25, and only the middle section of the pocket is shown in the diagram below.

Colours

Two strands of embroidery floss were used throughout, in the following colours: navy blue, royal blue, cornflower blue, mid blue, turquoise, pale turquoise, aqua, pale blue, and red.

To make up

Follow the general instructions for the 'Construction of the Pocket' (page 11), then attach it to the shirt.

To finish off

Feather-stitch the collar following the instructions on page 56, using 1 strand of each colour.

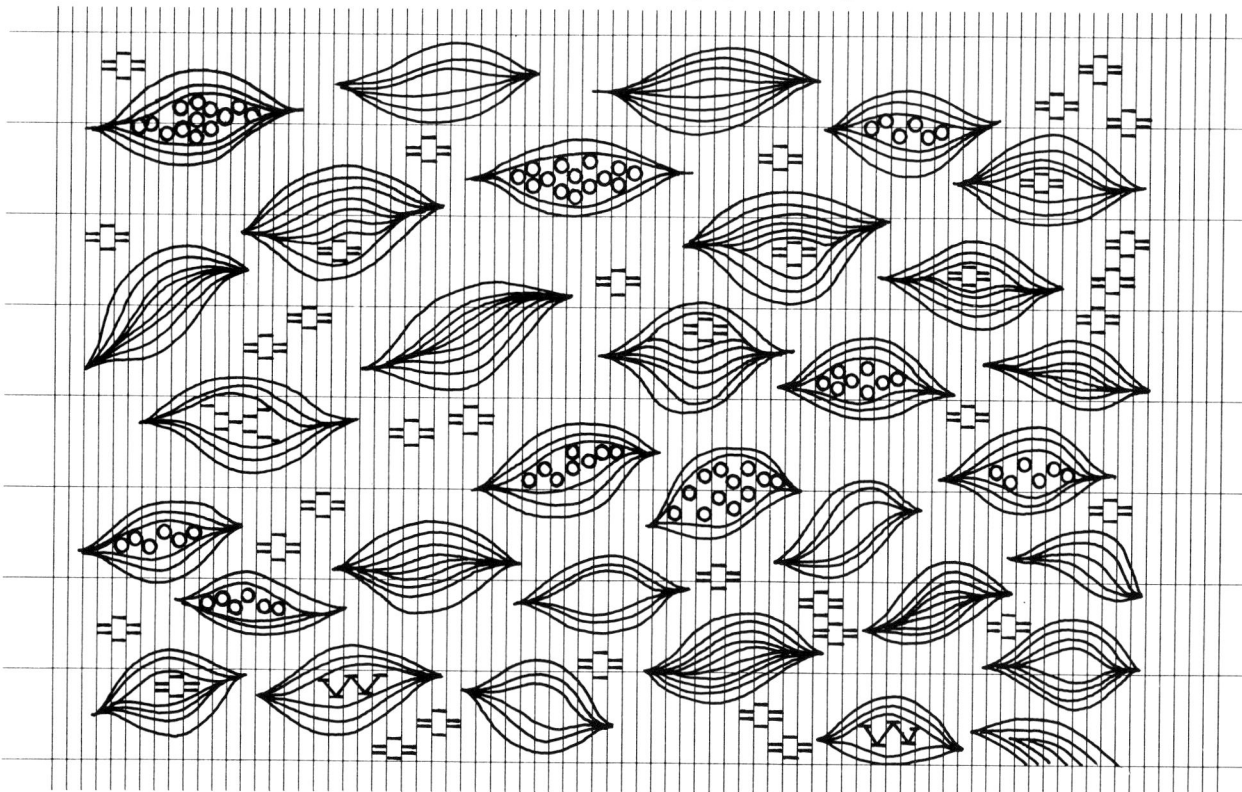

Bottle-green Shirt

Chambray Shirt

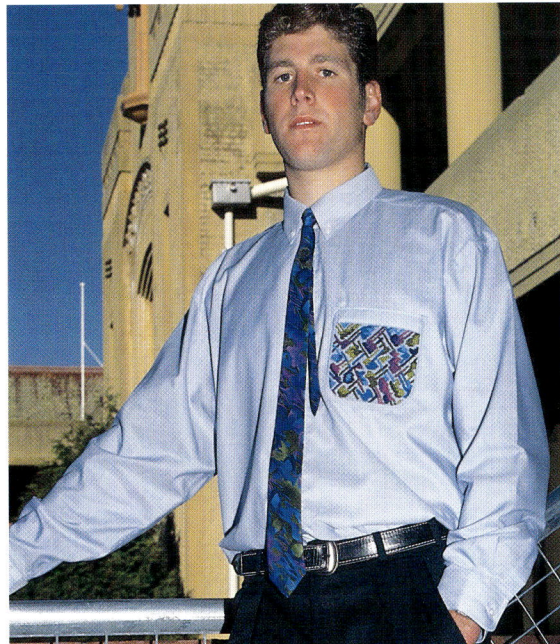

3

Kids' Gear

The beauty of smocking for children is that each project is smaller than its adult cournterpart: pockets for shirts, jeans, dungarees, shorts or dresses can be quite small tasks, so for a first project this aspect has considerable appeal.

The colours and boldness of design in Jigsaw smocking seem an ideal combination with denim and for practical and fashionable clothing for children, it is hard to go past this fabric.

The braces can be teamed with trousers, jeans or skirts, and will 'dress up' an otherwise casual outfit. They can be easily adapted to adult sizes: simply increase the amount of ribbon for each brace to provide the extra length required.

For variation, the playsuit could quite easily be changed to a pinafore by swapping a skirt for the shorts. This could be made of denim and then be worn just as it is on a hot day, with a T-shirt under it on a cooler day, and a skivvy or jumper under it in cold weather: a very versatile garment. Team a jaunty hat with matching smocked band to the smocked pinafore, and you will certainly have the most stylish 'kid on the block'.

The projects in this chapter are just a beginning, and are only intended as a starting point for the creative smocker.

These Dungarees are made from a Burda Pattern No. 4622, sizes 12m, 18m, 2, 3, and 4. There was a square pocket on the front, so I substituted a rounded smocked pocket to reflect the fabric turn-ups at the bottom of the legs. This idea could be used on any other Overall/Dungarees pattern.

Materials

Just for the pocket you need:

- A piece of chambray, denim or a similar weight fabric of 13 cm deep by 90 cm wide.
- Sufficient bias binding or fabric, cut into bias strips, to bind the pocket.
- A small piece of iron-on interfacing.

Pleating

Pleat 12 rows, including the top and bottom holding rows, and leave 2 pleats unsmocked at each end.

Smocking

No back-smocking is required.

Except for several small areas, which are left unsmocked, the entire pocket is stitched in Stacked Cables. This gives great freedom to change colours in different places so that you finish up with an 'original' design – a very satisfying achievement.

Just to add a distinctive touch, I have broken the angular lines of the design by using balls of yellow colour at irregular intervals.

Complete each shape before moving on to the next one. Keep the stitching very even, so that each row of Cable can be traced from one side of the smocked panel to the other, no matter how many colour changes are made.

Colours

Use 3 strands of embroidery floss throughout, in the following colours: yellow, orange, red, pink, violet, purple, royal blue, turquoise, aqua, light green, deep green, and black.

To make up

See the general instructions for the 'Construction of the Pocket' on page 11.

When complete, attach the pocket to the dungarees.

Diagram

This project does not require you to follow a stitch diagram. Just turn to page 28 and follow the arrangement of colours on the pocket of the dungarees.

Black Shirt

White Shirt

This is a ready-made shirt which I bought to go with baggy shorts which I had already made. To turn these two pieces of clothing into a set, I removed the original pocket but used it as a pattern for the new pocket.

You probably know that denim comes in every imaginable shade of blue, and trying to match the one you want is just about impossible. To overcome this difference in shades, I bound the pocket with the shorts' fabric, so that the eye is no longer aware of any colour discrepancy.

Materials

Just for the pocket you need:
- A piece of chambray or denim, 13 cm deep by 55 cm wide.
- A bias strip, cut from contrasting fabric, to bind the pocket.
- A small amount of iron-on interfacing.

Pleating

Pleat 12 rows, including the top and bottom holding rows, and leave 2 pleats unsmocked at each end.

Smocking

No back-smocking is required.

Almost the entire pocket has been stitched in Stacked Cables in this design, with just several small sections left unsmocked. As focal points, small yellow balls of colour appear at irregular intervals.

Keep the stitching very even so that each row of Cable can be traced from one side to the other on the smocked panel, no matter how many colour changes you make.

Complete each shape before moving on to the next one.

Colours

Use 3 strands of embroidery floss throughout, in the following colours: yellow, pink, red, violet, purple, blue, aqua, light green, deep green, and black.

To make up

See the general instructions for the 'Construction of the Pocket' on page 11.

When complete, attach the pocket to the shirt.

Diagram

This project does not require you to follow a stitch diagram. Just turn to page 29 and follow the arrangement of colours on the pocket of this shirt.

This is a Cherry Williams Pattern, size 3-7, available by mail order through Country Bumpkin in Adelaide. I made a Size 4, using stretch-knit fabric.

The smocked insert required a width of 115 cm but if it is to fit any other than a size 3 or 4 child, extra width is required.

Other playsuit patterns are also suitable. The insert fits with its lower edge at the waistline and its upper edge in the bodice. Make allowance for this when cutting out the playsuit.

Materials

Just for the insert you need:
- A piece of Homespun, pure cotton, or similar fabric of 10 cm deep by 115 cm wide.
- Some bias binding, sufficient to bind the top and bottom of the insert.

Pleating

Pleat 8 rows, including the top and bottom holding rows, and leave 2 pleats unsmocked at each end.

Smocking

Row 2: cable 4 rows, using a different colour for each row.

Row 7: cable 4 rows in reverse colour order.

Rows 3, 4, 5, and 6: Stack Cables in small squares, each of 6 Cables, beginning with an Over Cable and working 6 rows. Complete each square before starting the next. Keep the stitching very even, so that the rows remain straight.

Back-smocking is not required for this project.

Colours

Three strands of each embroidery floss is used throughout, in the following colours: red, yellow, purple, green, and blue.

To make up

Cut 2 lengths of bias binding to fit the lower edge of the bodice.

Pin the insert to the ironing board at the centre of the work and block to size of piping, then steam.

Pin the piping to the insert along the top row of smocking and machine-stitch it into position. Repeat this for the bottom of the insert. Remember to allow a 1.5 cm seam on all sides.

Make up the playsuit according to your pattern.

Diagram

This project does not require you to follow a stitch diagram. Just turn to page 32 and follow the arrangement of colours on the playsuit.

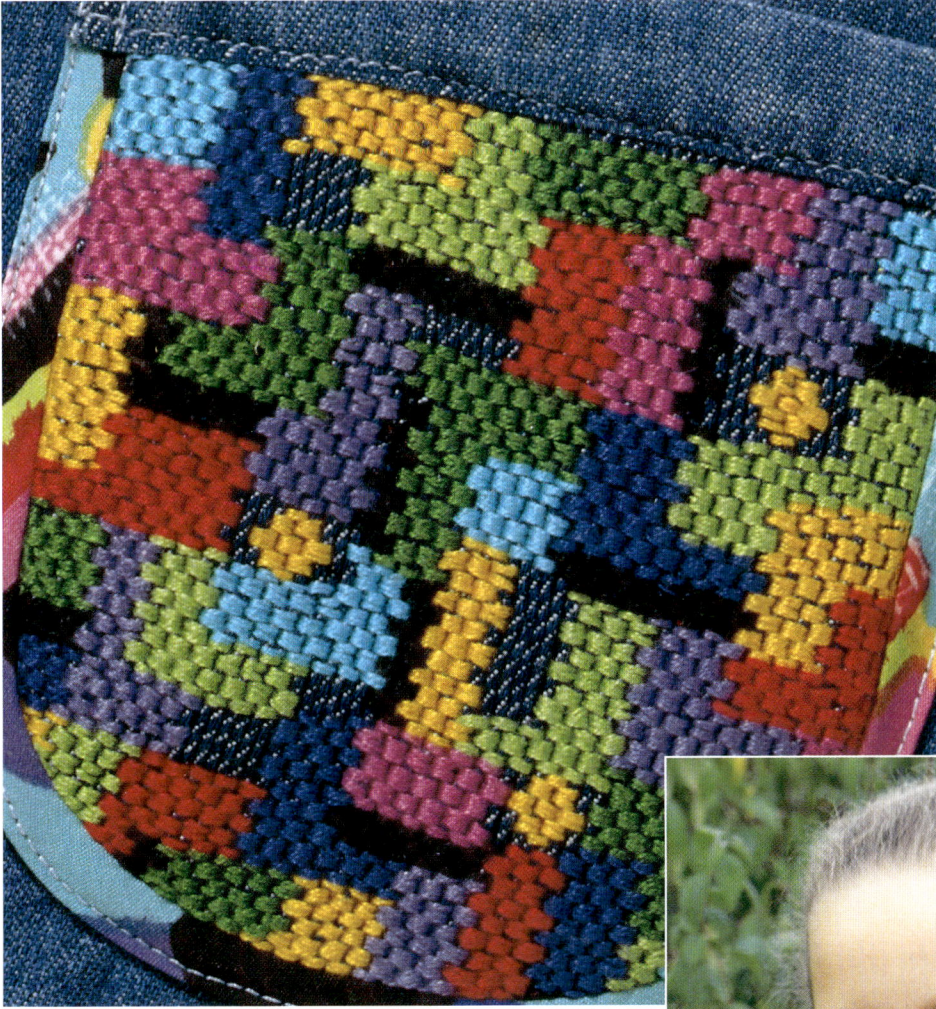

Denim Shirt

9 Braces

These braces can be worn with skirts or jeans. A back or front pocket could also be smocked to match. They are suitable for men and women as well as children. Just adjust the size by adding to the length of the ribbon. Brace fittings are available at most Sewing Supplies shops with varying clip sizes to suit the width of the elastic or ribbon.

Materials

To fit size 8-10, you need for each brace:
• A ribbon of 3.5 cm wide by 3.5 m long.
• Embroidery floss.

Pleating

Draw up 7 half-space rows, centred along the length of the ribbon. Leave 2 pleats unsmocked at either end and paint the ends with Fray Check to prevent fraying.

Smocking

Back-smock the back of the work on Rows 1, 4 and 7 using single rows of Cable.

Turn to the front and smock, following the diagram below, and using 3 strands of embroidery floss.

When complete, remove the gathering threads.

To make up

Using shirring elastic, reinforce the smocking to give greater strength and stretch by running a gathering line just below Rows 1 and 7, picking up each pleat on the back of the ribbon. Take care not to stretch the elastic whilst you are sewing.

Matching the smocking design, attach the brace fittings to the front of the smocking on both sections of the braces.

To complete the back, cross one brace over the other, approximately 11 cm back from the end of the final smocking shape, and stitch them in place. This join can be covered on both the front and the back of the braces with small diamond shapes, cut from vinyl or leather, to give a good finish. Complete the ends by attaching the brace fittings.

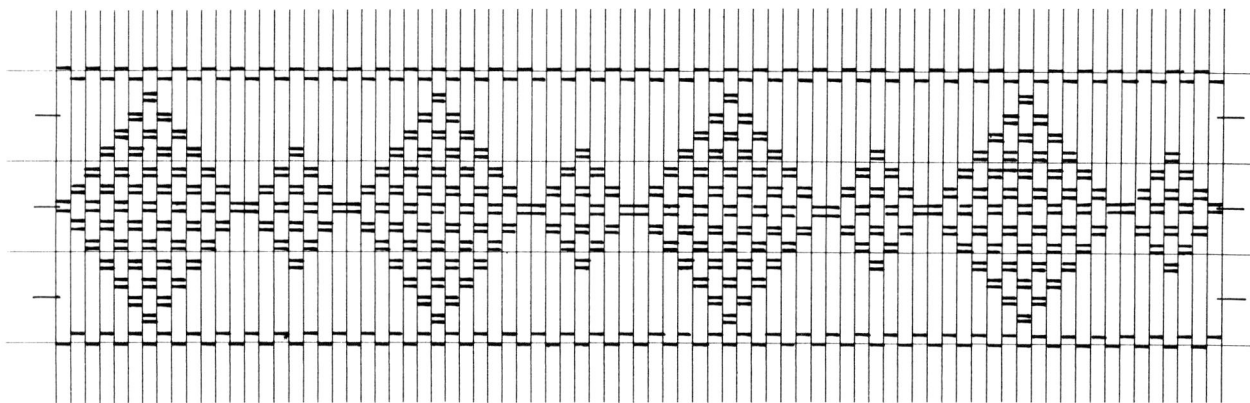

4

Anything Goes

The adaptability of smocking in general, and Jigsaw smocking in particular, will be quite obvious to the person who wishes to try this craft, but does not wish to make clothes. Once again, the possibilities seem endless, and the suggestions in this chapter are only meant as a starting point.

For a variation on the Guest Towel, the same idea could be enlarged and used on a bath towel, or pale colours could be chosen for the smocking and a beautiful, very personal gift for a new baby could be made.

The Wall Hanging could be smocked in brightly coloured geometric shapes and, teamed with a colourful fabric for a child's room, could be both

decorative and educational. Fabrics and colours chosen for a wall hanging could form the basis for the complete colour scheme of a room, or could form the focal point in the decoration of a favourite room.

The Earrings and Covered Buttons offer enormous potential for further ideas, different colour schemes and additional use of beads, as does the Hat Band. These small projects offer great opportunities for experimentation in both design and colour.

Allow your own creativity to lead you in new directions as you embark on these ideas.

Playsuit

Braces

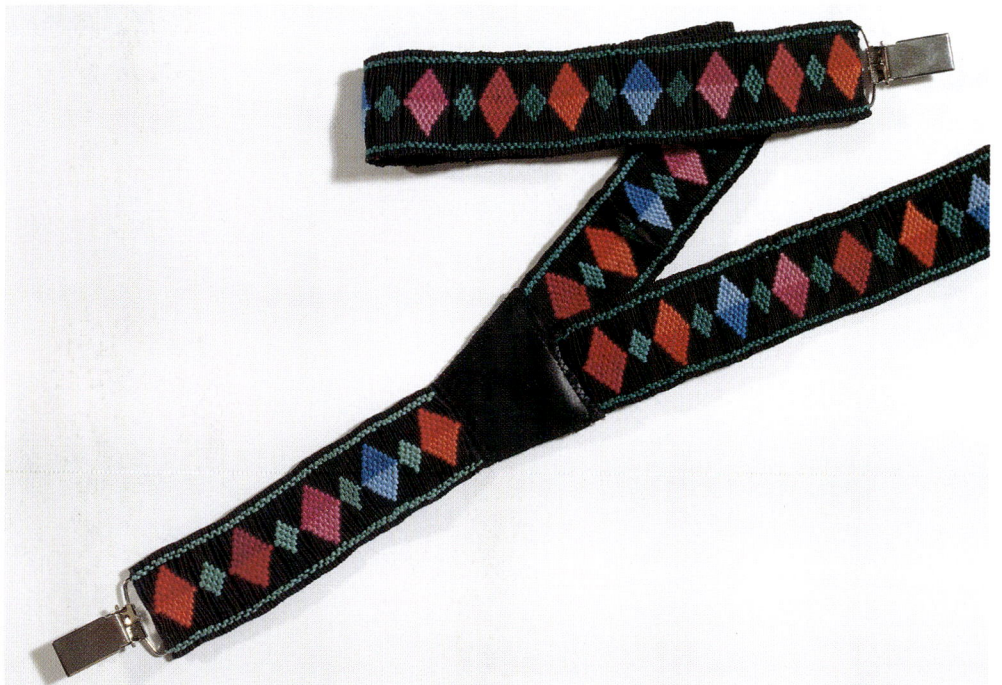

This guest towel makes a wonderful gift, is a great home decorator item, and offers an opportunity for trying out design and colour ideas on a small project. Any design in this book could easily be adapted to fit the smocked band.

Materials
- A hand towel.
- A ribbon of 3.5 cm wide by 1.75 m long. Satin or nylon ribbon is suitable, but the ribbon must be washable.
- Embroidery floss.

Pleating
Pleat 8 half-space rows, centring along the length of the ribbon. Apply Fray Check to the ends of the ribbon to prevent fraying. Leave 2 pleats unsmocked at both ends for the hems.

Smocking
Use 3 strands of embroidery floss throughout.
Row 1: Cable – beginning and ending with Over Cables.

Row 8: Cable – beginning and ending with Under Cables.

Upper Pyramid
Begin the first pyramid with 21 Cables, beginning and ending with Over Cables. Decrease by one stitch at each end of the pyramid on each row until one stitch remains. Shade floss from deep to medium to pale, changing each 4th and 7th row. Leave 3 Cables, then begin the second pyramid.

Lower Pyramid
The first lower pyramid will be a half pyramid. Begin with an Over Cable, cable 10.
Continue, following the diagram below, changing the floss shades on rows 4 and 7.
Miss 3 Cables, then continue as for upper pyramids.

To make up
Remove gathering threads and stretch gently to fit the towel. Either hand stitch or machine-stitch the ribbon to the towel.

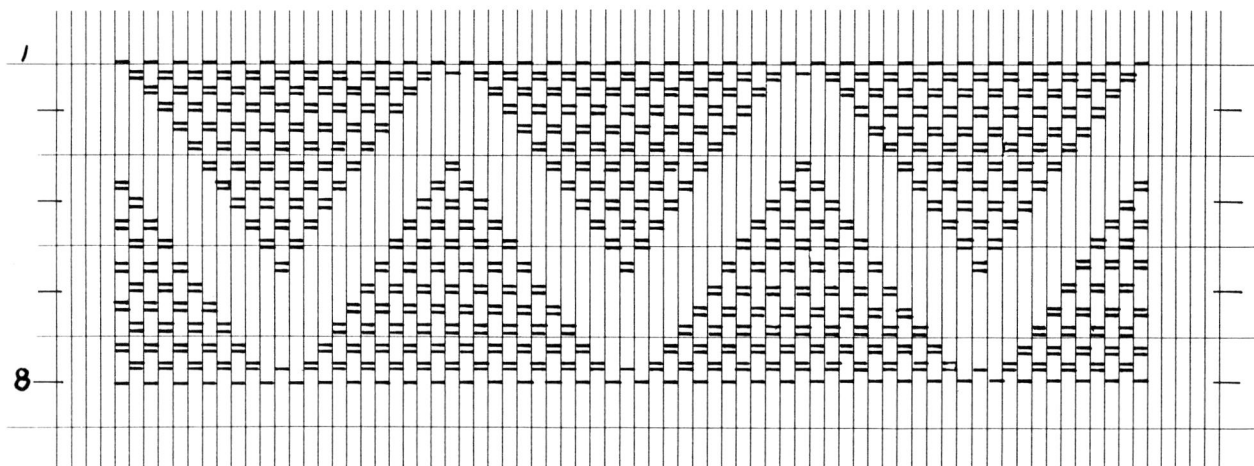

These napkin rings make lovely gifts and are good home decorator ideas too. They also present an ideal opportunity to try out different design ideas. There is no need to use the same design for each one. You could make the link by using the same colour combinations.

Materials

- A piece of poly-cotton fabric of 5 cm deep by 75 cm wide.
- A ribbon to match the fabric, of 4.5 cm wide by 15 cm long.
- Iron-on interfacing of 6 cm deep by 16 cm long

Pleating

Pleat 8 half-space rows, centred along the length of the fabric.

Smocking

Back-smock the centre 4 rows of gathering on the back of the work.

Turn to the front and follow the patterns in the diagrams below, using 2 strands of embroidery floss throughout.

Pattern 1

This is made up of Double Flowerettes spaced quite regularly along the length of the fabric, bounded by 3 rows of Cable on each of rows 1 and 8.

Pattern 2

This design is made up of small angular shapes fitting into one another, and is also bounded by several rows of Cable on rows 1 and 8.

To make up

Apply interfacing to the back of the smocking. Cut bias strips of fabric 16 cm long by 5 cm wide. With the right sides together, attach the bias strips to the smocking along the long edges, keeping the stitching line close to the first Cable row. Trim the seams back to 0.75 cm, and join the ends to make a ring. Working from the inside, fold over bias and tack into place.

Join the ribbon to make a ring. Slip over the smocked ring, wrong sides together, and slip-stitch it in place to cover the raw edges of the bias strips.

Turn to right side.

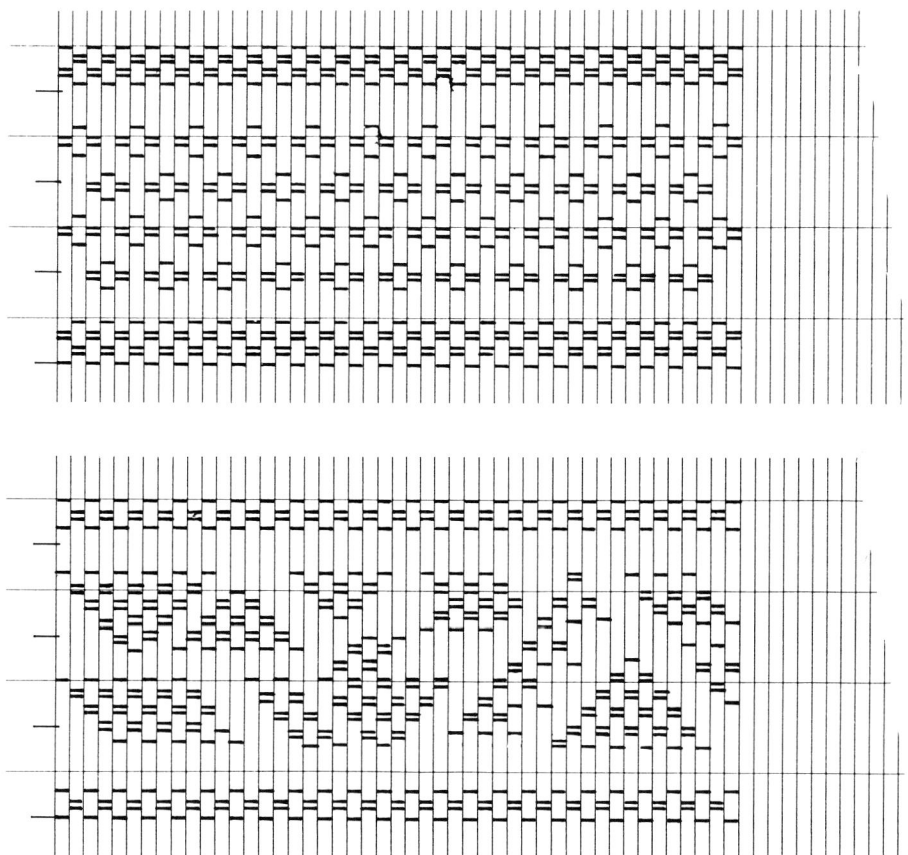

Guest Towel

Napkin Rings

With the information now available to us on skin care, hats have become an essential part of summer clothing, no matter how fashions may change. This opens up a new avenue for small smocking projects as hat bands are easily interchangeable: they just stretch over the crown of the hat. This offers great opportunities for trying out design ideas and for matching special outfits. You can't have too many hat bands!

Materials
- A ribbon of 2 m x 3.5 cm. Satin ribbons are very effective, and velvet ribbons are lovely with a winter outfit, though any type of ribbon is suitable.
- Embroidery floss to match the project.

Pleating
Pleat 8 half-space rows, centring along the length of the ribbon.

Apply Fray Check to the ends of the ribbon to prevent fraying. Leave two pleats unsmocked at either end for the seam.

Smocking
Back-smock, with single rows of Cable, rows 3, 4 and 5, using 3 strands of embroidery floss. Turn to the front.

Row 1: Cable – beginning and ending with Over Cables.

Row 8: Cable – beginning and ending with Under Cables.

Diamonds
Beginning on row 4.5 with Under Cable, cable 9. Complete a half diamond by reducing by one stitch at each end until only one stitch remains. Fasten off.

Note the colour changes in the lower half of the diamond (see the photographs on page 40).

Miss one pleat between each diamond and complete the length of ribbon.

To make up
Join the ends, carefully matching the centres of the diamonds and neaten the seam.

The band will now slip over the hat.

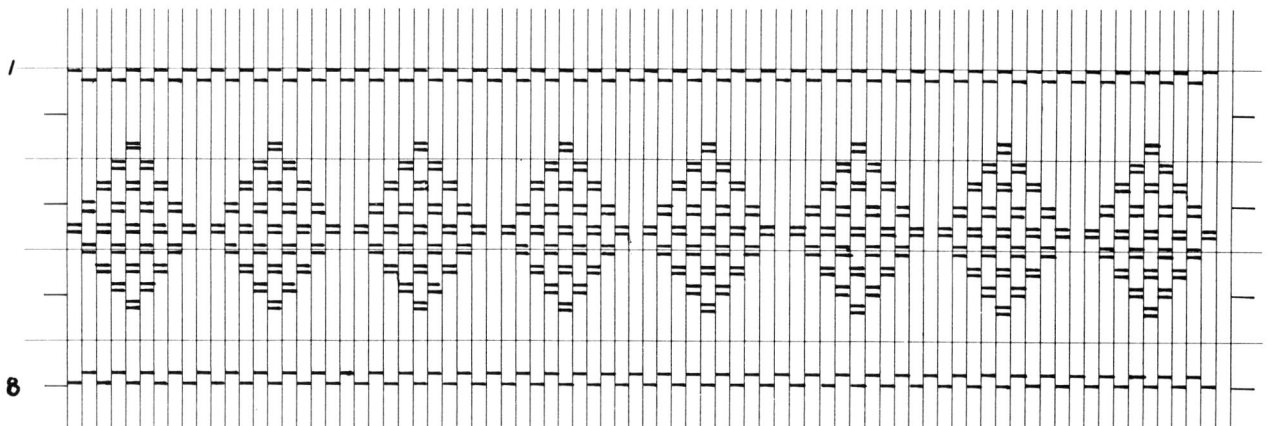

These small sampler bags make lovely gifts and are good projects for attempting Jigsaw smocking for the first time. It also gives you a chance to try your hand at designing your own patterns – patterns which may then lead to larger projects. The construction of the lavender bag is not unlike that of the pocket.

Having tried the lavender bag, you may like to vary it a little and make a rose bag. Use pink fabric and smock it in many shades of pink, then fill it with scented rose petals.

Materials
- A piece of homespun fabric or similar of 14 cm deep by 50 cm wide.
- A small amount of lace trim.
- Ribbon.
- Bias binding.

To prepare
Turn in a small hem at the top edge of the fabric and attach the flat lace.

Pleating
Pleat 10 rows, leaving two pleats unsmocked at each end.

Smocking
Back smock, with 2 strands of matching floss, each of the 10 gathering rows with single rows of Cable. Turn to the front and complete the Jigsaw smocking design, using 3 strands of embroidery floss throughout.

To make up
Gently press the smocking on the back. Cut the back of the bag to the same depth and width as the smocked panel, including seam allowances. Finish the top edge of the back panel with lace to match the front.
Join back and front, with wrong sides together, rounding the bottom of the bag for easier application of the binding. Trim the seam to 0.75 cm. With the front facing, attach the bias binding to the edges. Turn to the back and hand-stitch the binding into place.

Place a small bag of lavender in the smocked bag. Gather in the top with a gathering thread and tie off. Finish with ribbon trim.

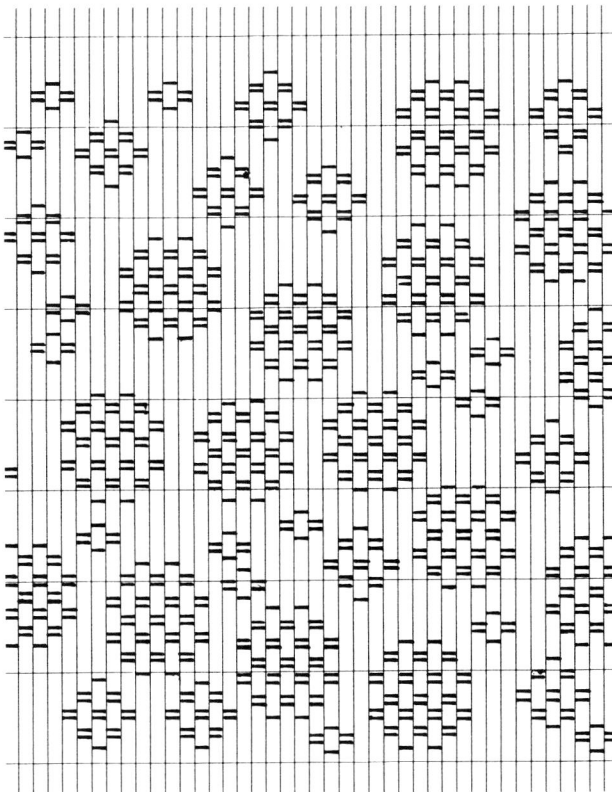

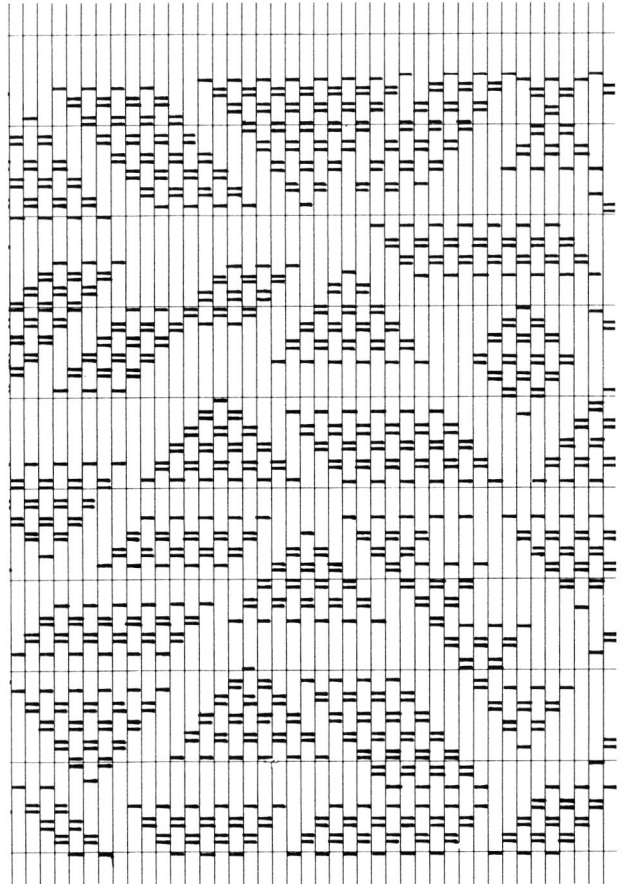

Hat Band

Lavender Bags

This project is most versatile. The 'buttons', once made, can be used in a great many ways. As a top button on a blouse, it makes an eye-catching feature. If used for all buttons it provides a colourful finish. Using them in either of these ways, it is best to make them as clip-on buttons which slip over normal shirt buttons. Another use for this covered button is to attach a brooch pin to it and wear it as a brooch or a lapel pin. A cluster of buttons could be used as a feature on an evening top.

Materials

- A piece of Georgette, voile, or silk of 8 cm deep by 60 cm wide is enough to make two 29 mm buttons.
- One card of 29-mm self-cover buttons.
- Embroidery floss, including gold/silver lurex thread.

Pleating

Pleat 10 half-space rows, using rows 1 and 10 as holding rows only.

Smocking

Back-smock each row of gathering, including the holding rows. It is necessary to do all this back-smocking to hold the fabric firmly when fitting the smocking around the button shape. Turn to the front and smock small triangles with Stacked Cables, following the diagram below. Do not remove the gathering threads at this stage.

Colours

Two strands of embroidery floss or single lurex thread were used throughout, in the following colours: red, green, turquoise, and gold.

To make up

Before removing the gathering threads, centre the button over the front of the smocking and draw around the button with a piece of tailor's chalk – to be rubbed off later. Using a small stitch, machine-stitch around this line.

Using a cardboard template (on the back of the card of buttons), trace the appropriate circle, again centring over the smocking. Machine-stitch round this circle.

Remove gathering threads, then cut very close to the outside edge of the larger machine-stitched circle.

Now follow the manufacturer's instructions for making buttons, taking care not to distort the smocked fabric when fitting it over the button.

This button can now be sewn directly onto the garment.

If it is to be attached to clip-on buttons, carefully cut off the shank on the back of the button with a sharp knife, glue a circle of felt to the back of the button to achieve a better fit when glueing it to a clip-on button.

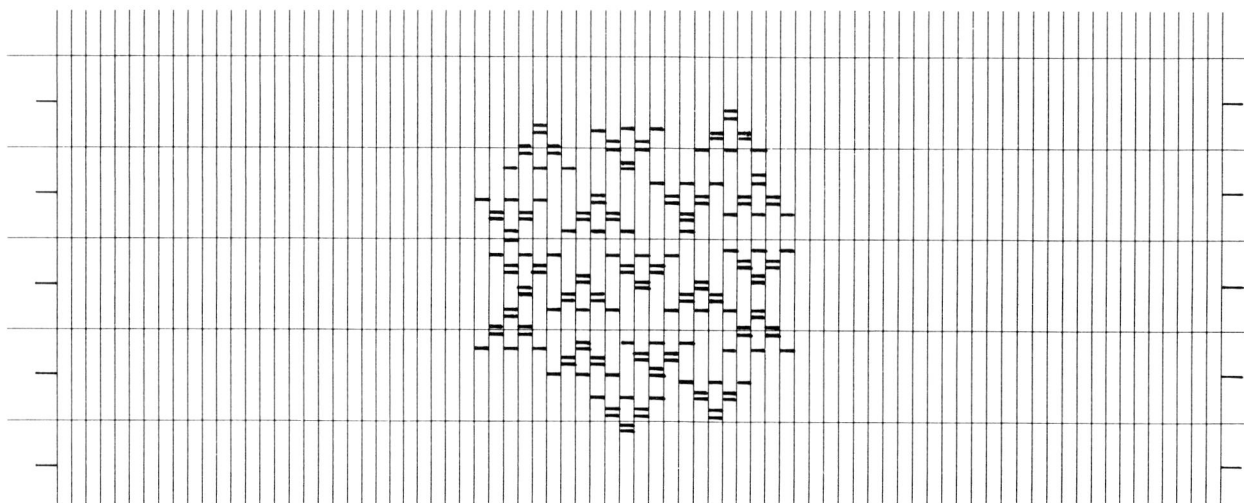

These earrings are designed for a special occasion, like a night at the theatre or a special dinner.

Materials

- A piece of Georgette, voile, or silk of 6.5 cm deep by 75 cm wide is sufficient for two earrings. Turn up a very fine double hem on one long edge.
- Embroidery floss, including gold and silver threads.
- Gold and/or silver beads.
- Earring fittings.
- An empty cotton reel spool (73 m thread size), cut in half.

Pleating

Pleat 7 half-space rows, keeping the first row as close as possible to the small hem. This will form a fine frill-like edge for the earrings. Leave two pleats unsmocked at either end.

Smocking

Smock, following the diagram below.

Colours

Two strands of embroidery floss were used throughout in the following colours: gold, silver and red.

To make up

Find the centre of smocking and machine-stitch two lines from top to bottom – 5 mm apart – then cut between the two lines to make two pieces of smocking. Remove the gathering threads. Hand-sew the ends together, matching the design on each piece of smocking to make two small cylinders to fit over cotton reel halves.

Run gathering thread around the top of the cylinder (raw edge) and draw up. Squeeze a line of fabric glue around the top of the cut end of the cotton reel, fit the smocking over, pulling the raw edge through the hole at the top of the reel, using gathering thread for this, and allow the glue to dry to hold it in place.

Glue a circle of felt to cover the bottom end of the cotton reel and oversew the gathering thread to this, to secure the raw edges inside the reel.

Thread the beads on strong cotton and attach them through the felt circle, up through the cotton reel, and oversew in fabric. Fasten off.

The gold cap covering the top of the earring is a small cap bought at a bead shop. This covers any rough edges left at the top, but a circle of felt could be either glued or stitched over to cover this.

Finally, attach earring fittings to suit pierced or un-pierced ears. These can be purchased at specialty bead shops or at most sewing supplies shops.

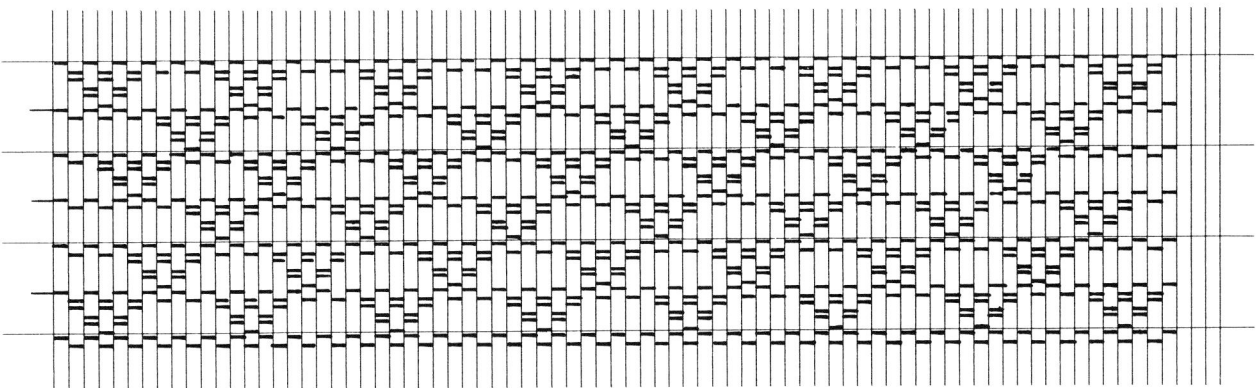

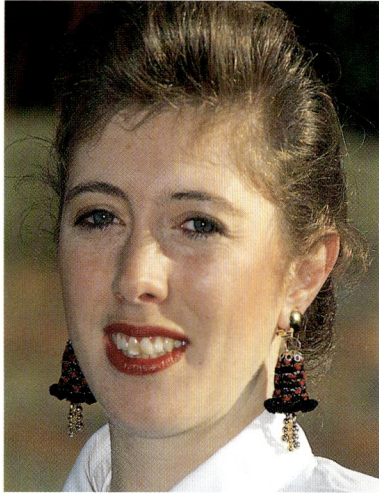

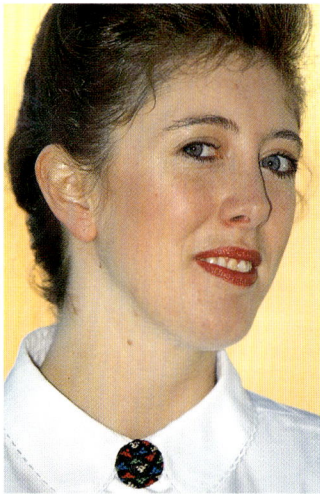

Earrings

Clip-on Buttons

Wall Hanging

The design in the smocking of this wall hanging could be used to match any floral patterned fabric and would only then require changes to the colours. Patterned velvet and other 'evening' fabrics offer vibrant colour waves for this smocking. Many furnishing fabrics are also ideal, particularly when you are matching an existing colour scheme in a home.

Materials

- A piece of black Homespun, or similar weight fabric of 21 cm deep by 85 cm wide
- A 45-cm length of patterned fabric, to be used both as an inspiration for the smocking and, eventually, as the covered mount or frame.

Pleating

Pleat 20 rows, using rows 1 and 20 as holding rows only. Leave 4 pleats unsmocked at either end.

Smocking

Using 3 strands of embroidery floss throughout in colours to suit your fabric, follow the diagram below for design ideas.

To make up

I purchased two cardboard mounts from an art supplies shop, a small one of 31.5 cm x 28.5 cm in black, and a large one of 34 cm x 30 cm. Each mount measures 6.5 cm from the inside edge to the outside edge.

Carefully centre the small frame over the smocking and glue it into position. Normally, when framing an embroidery, the work is stretched and laced over heavy cardboard. However, this is not appropriate for smocking! This is why substantial borders of fabric have been left on all sides of the smocking to allow for glueing it to the mount.

To prepare the large mount, cut the patterned fabric to fit this mount, leaving 3 cm hems on both the outside and inside edges of the frame. To reinforce the inside corners of the fabric, I painted small areas at each corner with Fray-check, then carefully cut in each corner to allow the fabric to be folded to the back of the frame/mount and glued into place. The outside edges of the fabric can now be folded firmly to the back of the frame/mount and glued into place. Check the front constantly to ensure the fabric is flat and no creases appear. Centre the larger mount over the smaller mount and glue in place. Attach hooks for hanging.

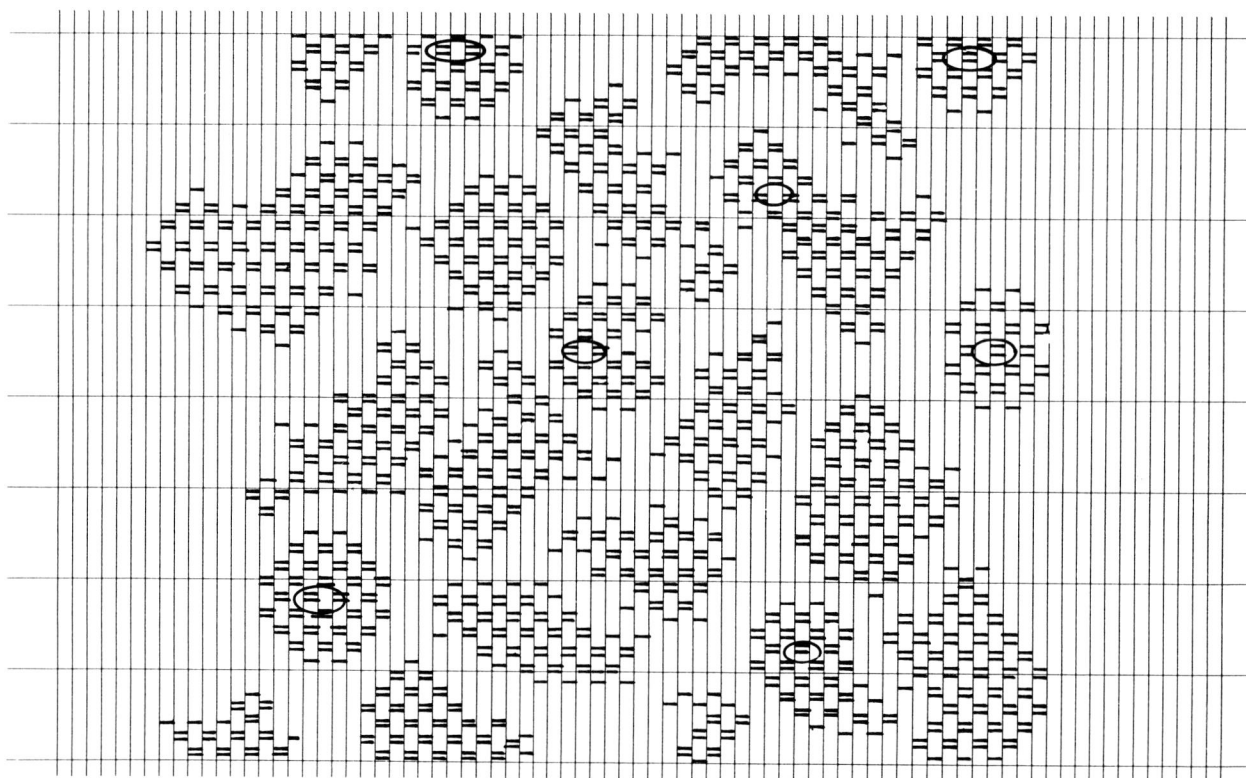

Stitch Descriptions

You will need the following stitches for 'jigsaw' smocking. There are, of course, many other smocking stitches, and for further instructions and information on these I recommend Margie Bauer's *Australian Smocking for Beginners*.

With all smocking it is important to remember to pick up each new pleat at the same level, keeping the needle horizontal. Changing the thread position will alter the look of the stitch.

Cables

I often use my top and bottom rows of cables (sometimes doing as many as five or six rows) to introduce colours I intend to use in the major pattern. This way, they not only perform the task of controlling the work at the top and bottom of the piece of smocking, but also give the opportunity to see how these colours are going to show up on your insert. Now is the time to make changes in colour schemes if you can see that the effect you were hoping for will not eventuate.

From three to six strands of cotton can be used to give a bold effect. I generally use three, though if you are working on finer materials you will probably find that two strands is more suitable.

Cable Stitch

This is the main stitch, used in a variety of ways in 'jigsaw' smocking, e.g. in borders, in geometric designs using stacked cables, and for

back-smocking. Each cable holds two pleats and you will be entering the pleat from the right and coming out on the left.

Begin with a single knot bringing the needle to the front of the material in the left hand side valley of the second pleat, a needle's width above the gathering row.

To begin a stitch, the needle comes through the left side of the first pleat. It is then inserted into the right side of the second pleat, coming out on the left side.

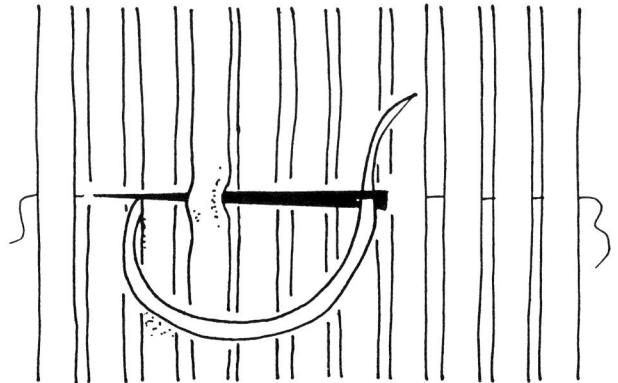

1 With the needle parallel to the gathering thread, pick up the second pleat with the thread under the needle. Give a gentle tug upwards as you finish the stitch. This forms an Under Cable.

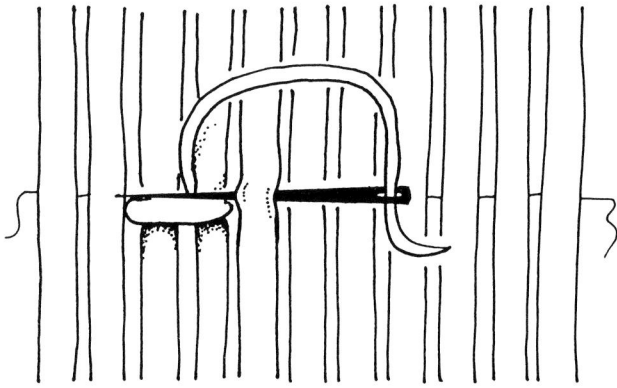

2   Now, with the thread over the needle, pick up the third pleat and gently pull the thread down as you finish the stitch. This is called an Over Cable.

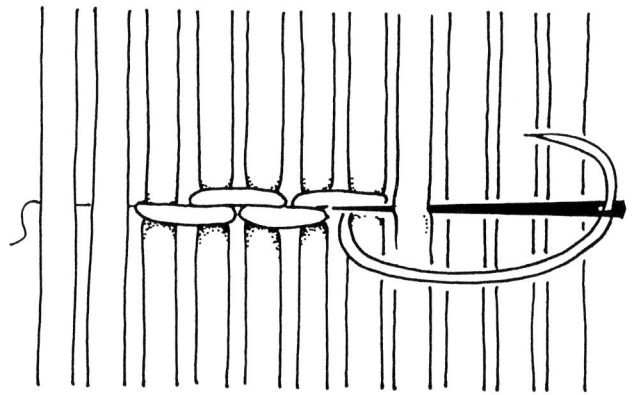

3   The needle enters each pleat at the same level, whether you're making an Under or an Over Cable. Don't move the needle, only the thread.

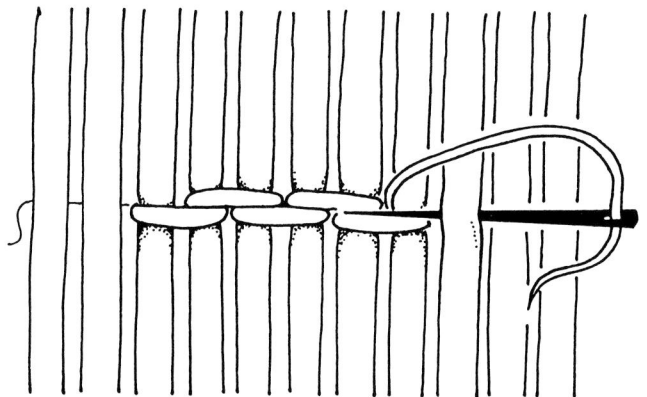

4   Pick up the fifth pleat with the thread over the needle.

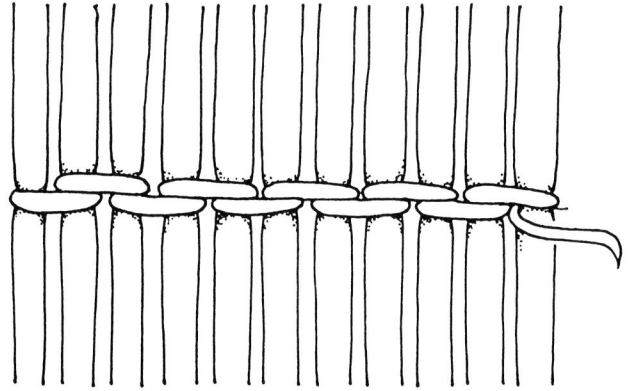

5   Pick up the sixth pleat with an Under Cable.

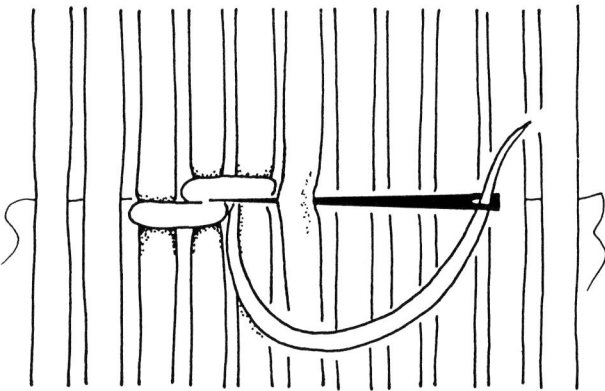

6   Pick up the seventh pleat with an Over Cable.

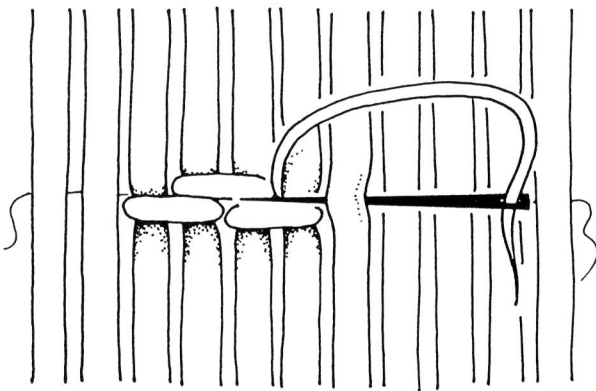

7   Continue across the row.

SMOCKING WITH A DIFFERENCE

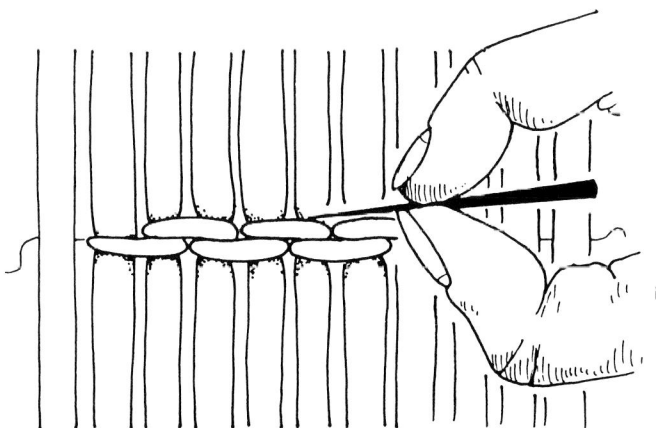

8 Sometimes you will see the stitches are not quite level. Straighten the tops of the stitches with the tip of your needle or fingernail.

Double Cable Stitch

Work one row of Cable Stitch. Begin with an Under Cable. Use the gathering thread as a guide.

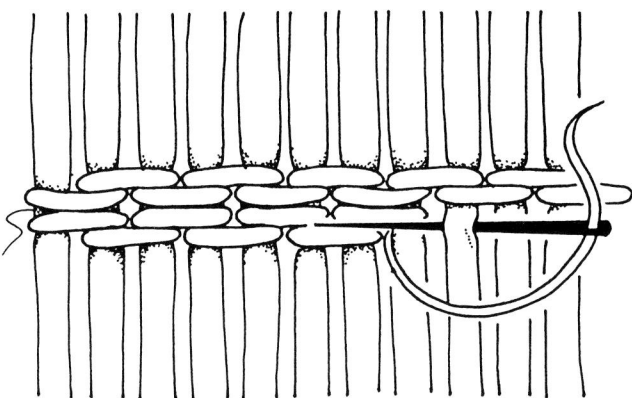

Start a second row of cables with an Over Cable. Work this row straight under the top row so the stitches touch each other but don't overlap. The two rows will give the effect of a chain.

Single Flowerettes

Flowerettes can be used in many designs. They add a lift to geometric designs. They consist of four Cable Stitches and require four pleats.

Strip your cotton for better coverage, pick up two-thirds of each pleat, work with a loose tension and straighten stitches with the eye of the needle.

The illustrations show two methods of making the Single Flowerette.

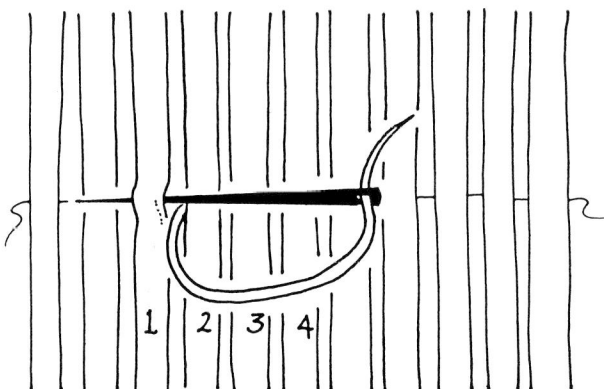

1 Bring the needle out in the valley between the first and second pleat. Insert the needle from right to left, two-thirds into the depth of the pleat.

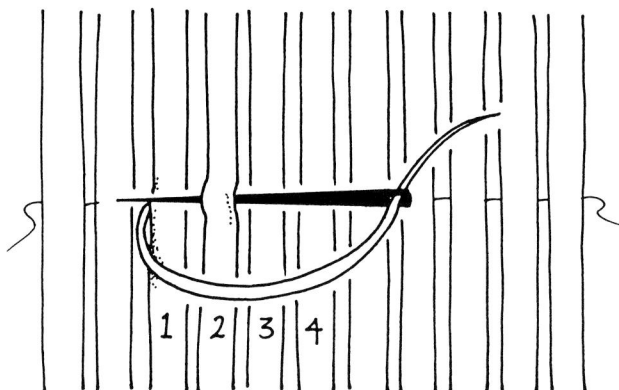

2 Pick up the second pleat with an Under Cable.

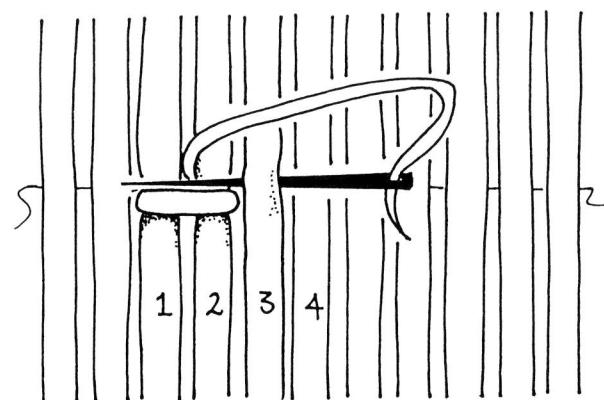

3 Pick up the third pleat with an Over Cable.

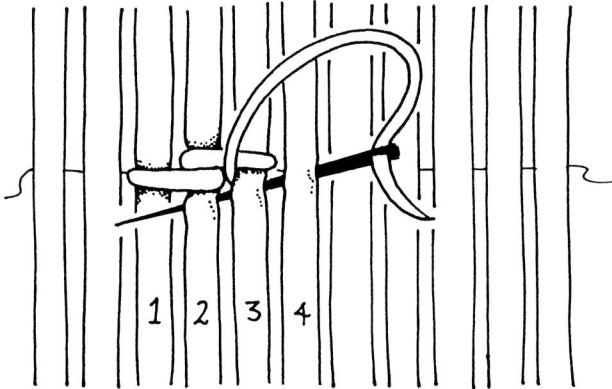

4   With thread over, take the needle back through the fourth, third and second pleats, re-emerging in the valley between the first and second pleat. Pull the thread through gently.

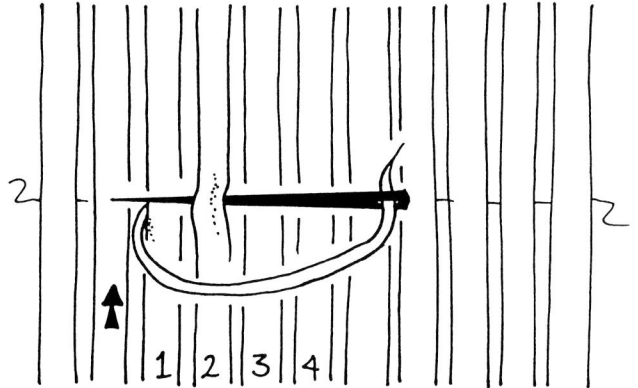

5   Pick up the third pleat again with an Under Cable.

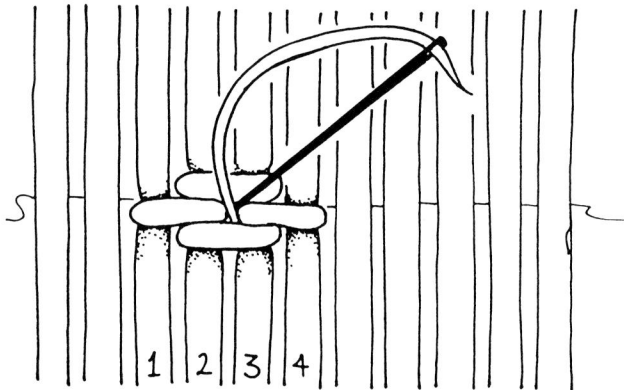

6   Finish off by pushing the needle back into the valley between the second and third pleat in the centre of the Flowerette. Pull the thread through, take a backstitch and tie-off.

Method Two
Bring the needle out in the valley between the first and second pleat. Insert the needle from right to left, two-thirds into the depth of the pleat.

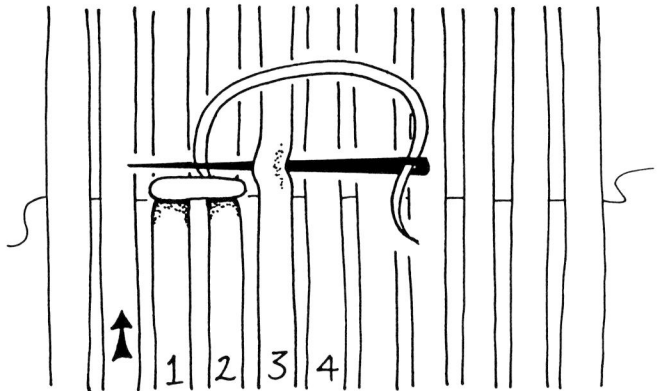

1   Pick up the second pleat with an Under Cable.

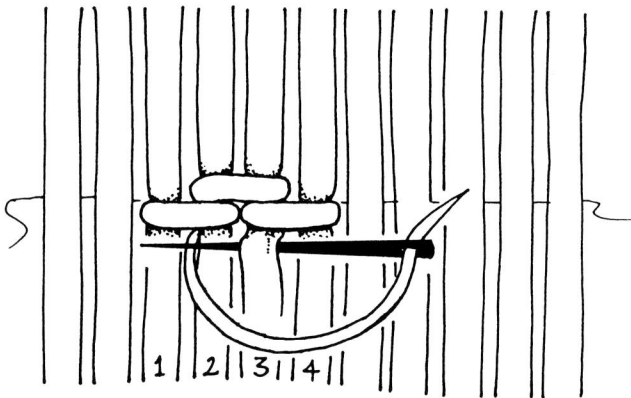

2   Pick up the third pleat with an Over Cable.

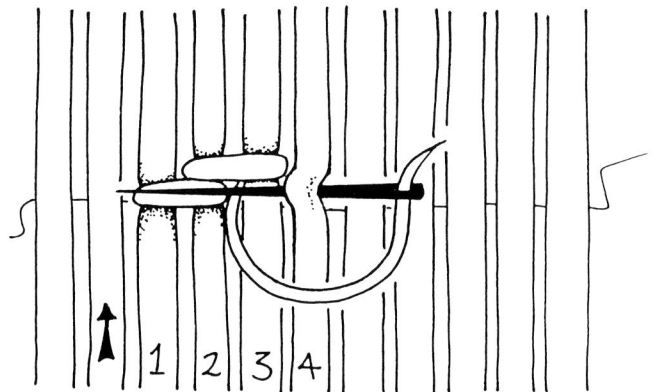

3   Pick up the fourth pleat with an Under Cable.

SMOCKING WITH A DIFFERENCE

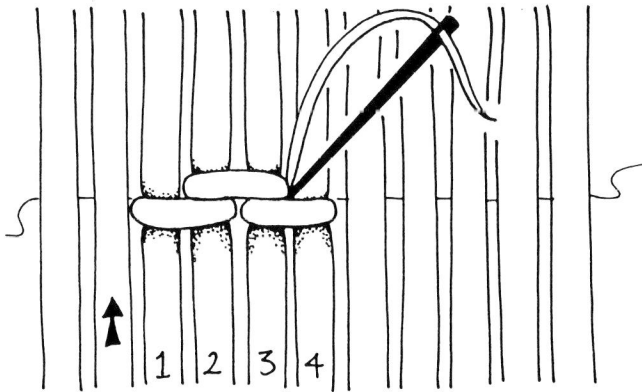

4 Push the needle to the back of your work exactly where it came out. Turn your work upside down.

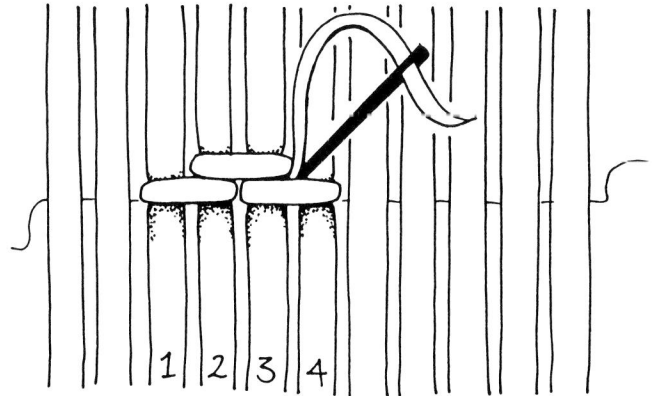

5 Make an Under Cable to correspond with the middle cable in the first row. Push the needle to the back, take a backstitch and tie off.

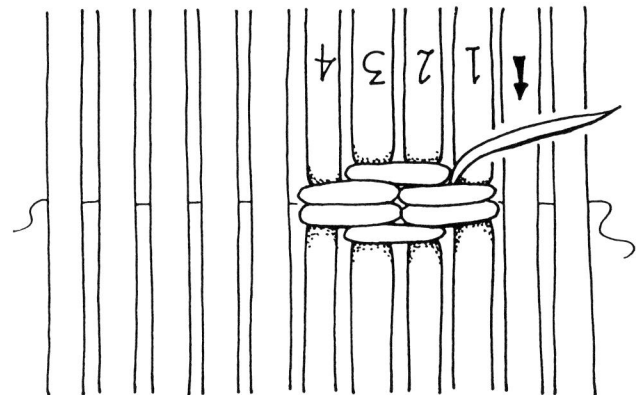

Double Flowerettes

Start as usual, and then:

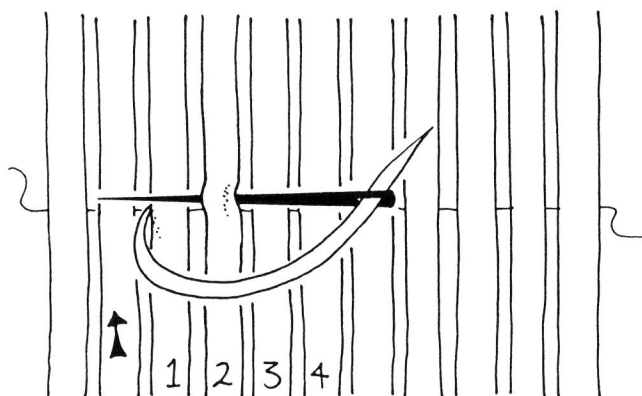

1 Take a level Cable Stitch with a thread under, picking up the second pleat.

2 Push the needle to the back of your work, exactly where it came out.

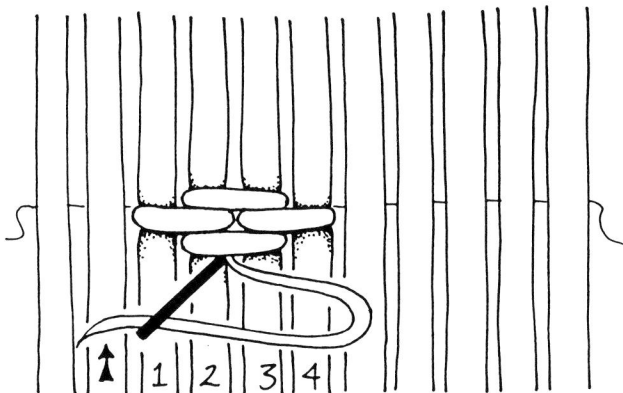

3 Turn the work upside down, and directly above your last stitch, repeat with three cables (Under, Over, Under). Take the needle to the back, make a backstitch and tie off.

Stacked Cables

Stacking cables takes practice to perfect but is not really difficult. It is time consuming and you will find that this type of smocking is a lot slower than conventional smocking. However, I feel the dramatic effects which can be achieved far outweigh any of the drawbacks.

You soon learn where to place each row so that there are never any gaps. It is necessary for each stitch to 'kiss' the one above (just touching it, but without covering it). This is easily achieved by having only a needle's width between each row.

It is well worth practising on a sampler to achieve the desired results, so that when you actually work on your garment you are satisfied with the results.

Care must be taken at all times to watch your tension (looser than would be used for all other smocking stitches, but constant) or pleats will be pulled out of shape and the inset will develop a distorted appearance which will detract from the finished work. This requires care particularly with the first and last cables in each row of stacking – once again, worth a little practice and patience!

As in picture smocking, stacked cables are purely decorative, providing visual impact, whilst the back-smocking is the functional stitch.

Stacking cables

This smocking method involves working a single row of Cable Stitches, building out from that row to create shapes. There are two kinds of stacked cables: Pyramids and Stacked Rectangles/Squares.

With Pyramids, each row is decreased or increased by a stitch at either end. Stacked Rectangles/Squares are worked by turning your work upside down at the end of each row and stitching a mirror image of the previous row.

Stacked Rectangles always have one free pleat left on either end. This can be quite effective, but sometimes you will want a smooth edge to your work, in which case you stitch a couple of single satin stitches over this one pleat.

This type of smocking is most effective using stranded cotton. Usually three or four strands are sufficient. These strands can be stripped and re-grouped to give a fuller effect.

It is important to insert the needle at the same level for each stitch and to work with a slightly looser tension than normal.

Pick up two-thirds of each pleat when stacking cables and be consistent with both stitch depth and tension. Level the top of the stitches with your fingertips or needle. If possible, work the first row on a gathering line and build out from there.

If you have decided to graph your design, then find the widest row and use that as your base row.

Sometimes the thread will need to be separated again as you work. Try wiping the thread with 'Bounce' if it becomes tangled.

Be patient, work slowly and remember the top and bottom Cable Stitches sit on each other.

Stacked Pyramids

Stacked Pyramids are worked with an odd number of stitches over an even number of pleats.

(Remember, you pick up the second pleat with your first stitch.)

Look closely at a Stacked Pyramid and you will see you are decreasing each row by one stitch on either side and making a mirror image (opposite) of the previous row worked. In the illustration, we have stitched a row on nine cables and decreased to one cable. Sometimes, to achieve a sharp point on a Pyramid, you may find it necessary to finish with a single cable.

Begin the row by passing the needle from right to left in the first pleat. This is especially important in stacking cables as you can see the depth of the stitch each time and line up the next row accordingly. Pick up two-thirds of the pleat.

1   Stitch a row of nine cables, beginning with an Under Cable. Keep the stitches level and the tension a little looser than normal.

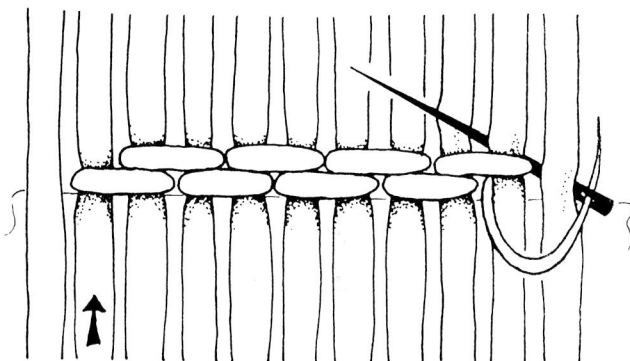

2   On the final Under Cable, point the needle up tot he next row and take it through two pleats. Bring the needle to the surface in the valley of the last Over Cable. Pull the thread through the fabric and turn the work upside down.

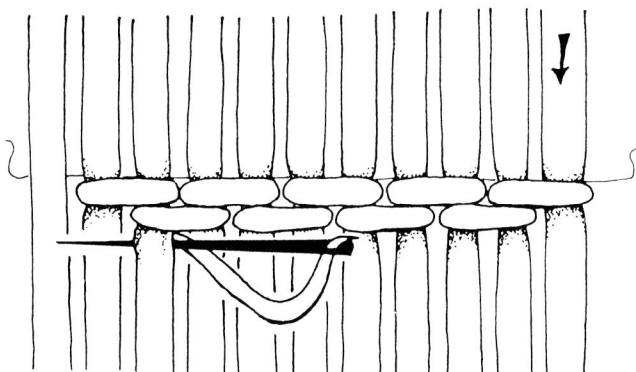

3   Begin the next row by passing the needle back from right to left in the first pleat. (You are already in position.) This will bring you exactly beneath the Over Cable in the first row you stitched.

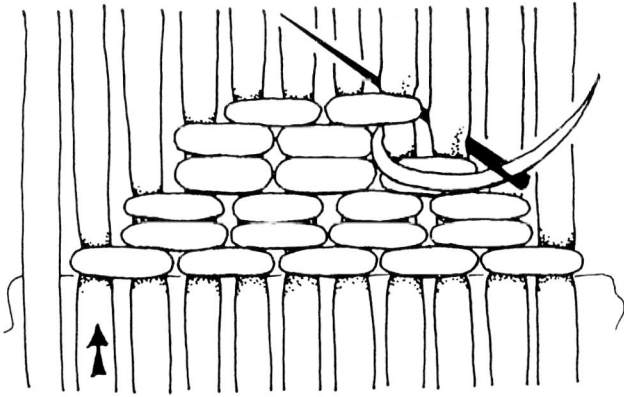

4   Work slowly and carefully. Remember you are decreasing each row by two stitches and you begin each new row with an opposite cable to the row before it.

Continue across this row and make seven cables, ending with an Over Cable. Point the needle up, picking up the last two pleats.

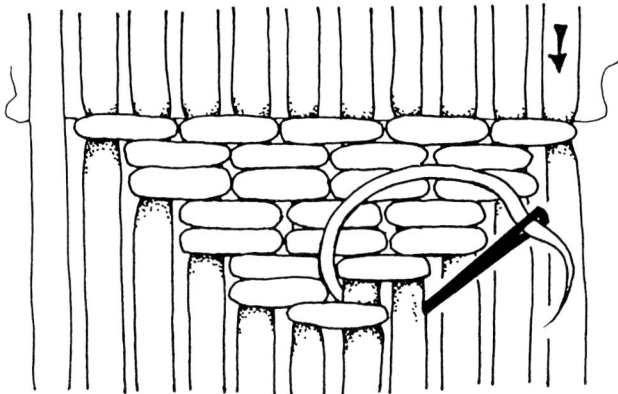

5   Turn the work around once you have positioned the needle exactly beneath the Over Cable in the first row. Make five cables.

Turn the work around and make three cables. Push the needle through to the back, take a backstitch and tie off.

Stacked Rectangles – filling in the gaps

Start by taking the needle from right to left in the first pleat.

Begin the row with an Under Cable. The illustration shows seven cables. Be sure you start and end each row with an Under Cable.

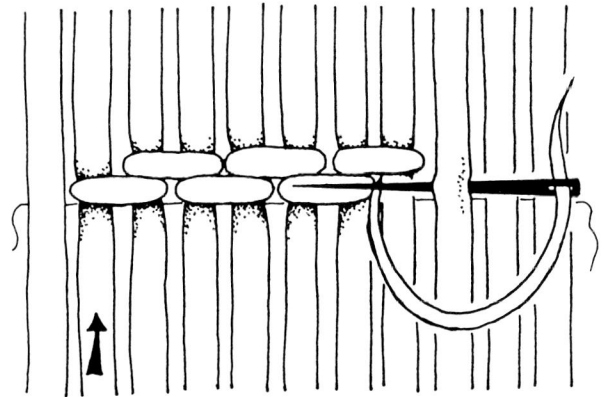

1   Make seven Cable stitches, finishing with an Under Cable.

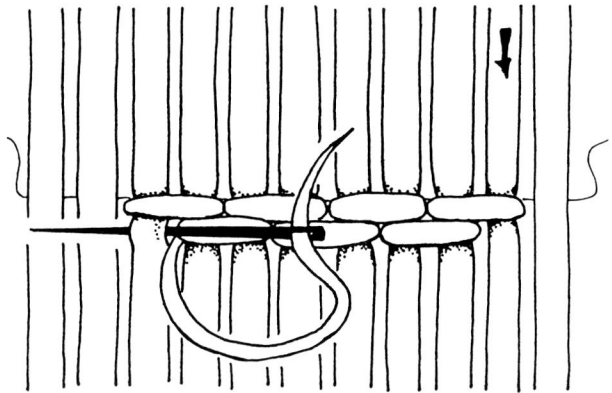

2   Turn your work upside down. Take the needle from right to left in that first pleat. Make sure the depth is consistent with the first cable you worked.

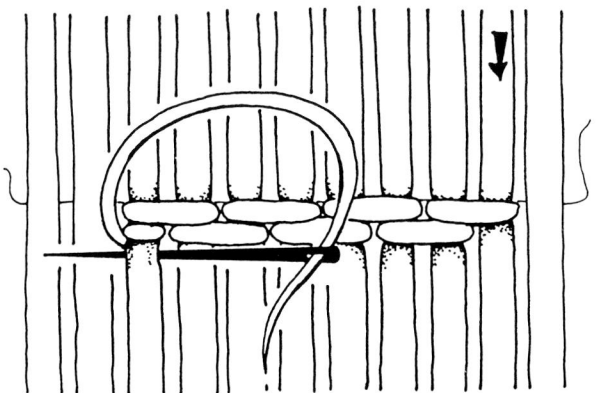

3   With thread over take two tiny satin stitches down in the same pleat a needle's width from each other. This fills the 'gap' left by two opposite cables. The last satin stitch should bring you down ready to start the next row.

STITCH DESCRIPTIONS

Begin the next row with an Under Cable and work a mirror image of the row before. Make seven cables, ending with an Under Cable. Work two tiny satin stitches over one pleat upwards to fill the gap.

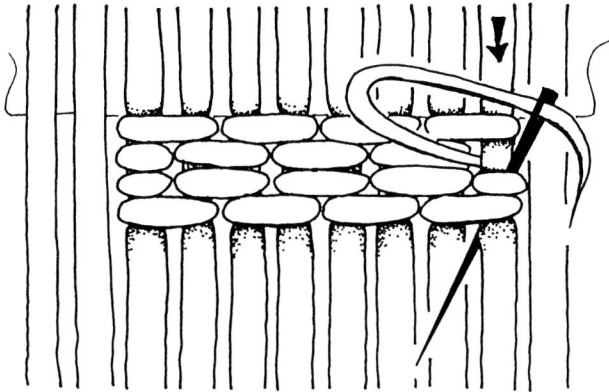

Make seven Cable Stitches beginning with an Under Cable. Finish with an Under Cable.

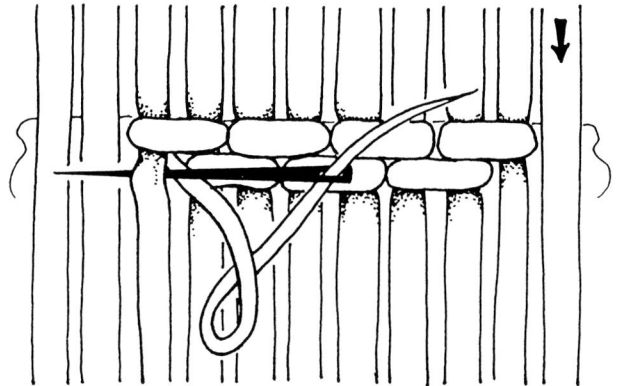

4 On the top satin stitch point the needle down through the last pleat and bring it out in the left valley of the same pleat, just in the middle of the final Cable Stitch.

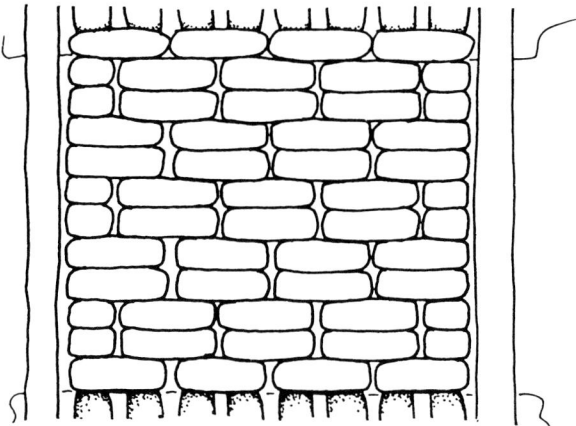

1 Turn the work upside down, and start the next row by stitching right to left in the first pleat a needle's width below the second cable on the row above. This brings you into line for your second row.

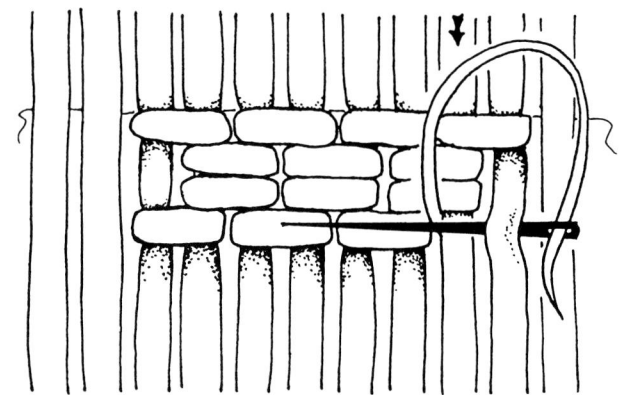

5 Turn the work around, take the needle from right to left in the first pleat. Keep making seven cables plus the satin stitches and continue building your blocks. Always begin and end the rows with an Under Cable.

Finish by pushing the needle through to the back on the right side of the last pleat, taking a backstitch and knotting the thread.

2 Pick up the second pleat with an Under Cable and work across the row. On your last Cable Stitch (which should be an Under Cable) flip the thread over to stitch it. This brings you into line for your third row.

Stacked Rectangles – leaving the gaps
Start by taking the needle from right to left in the first pleat. Remember, pick up two-thirds of the pleats, pick up each pleat at the same level, don't pull too tightly.

French Knots

These two stitches give another dimension to your smocking. Each can have a part to play in 'jigsaw' smocking. Combined with back-smocking, it is possible for the whole piece to be worked in either one, or in a combination of both.

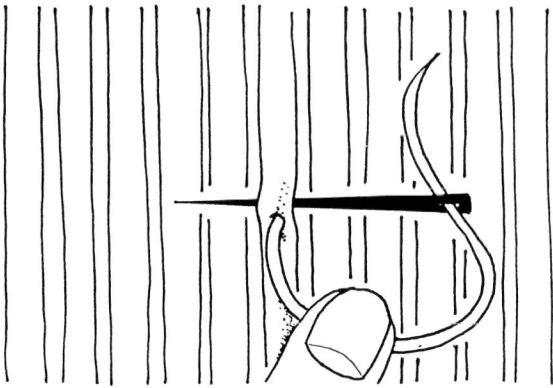

1 Insert the needle from right to left in a single pleat, just picking up the top and holding the thread under the needle with your left thumb.

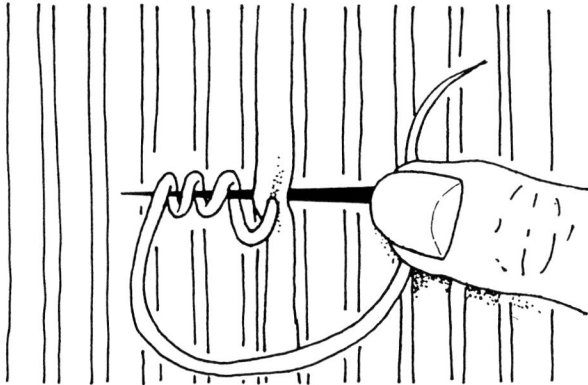

2 Hold the eye of the needle against the fabric with your right thumb. With your left thumb and forefinger, wrap the thread around the thicker part of the needle which is poking through. Wrap the thread toward you (left to right) two or three times. Don't wrap too tightly but be consistent.

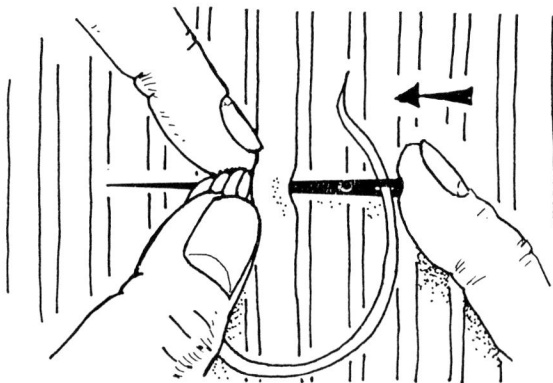

3 Push the needle eye through the fabric with your right thumb. At the same time, ease the knot down to the fabric with your left thumb and forefinger, keeping the thread windings tight.

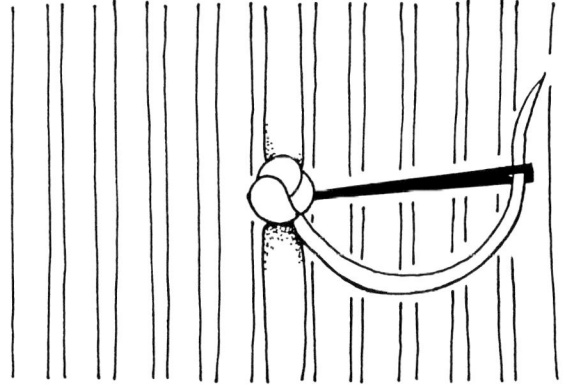

4 Pull the thread through, holding the knot down on the fabric. You will now have a little knot on the top of the pleat. Re-insert the needle close to where it first emerged. Take a backstitch on the wrong side of the material and tie off.

To make French Knots larger, try increasing the number of strands of thread rather than winding more wraps around the needle.

French Knots are also useful in picture smocking, where they can be used to depict eyes and noses.

Back-smocking

As the design you choose may not be ideal for elasticity or for holding the pleats evenly in place on the front, backsmocking assumes a very important role.

It is worked while the gathering threads are still in place in the material so that you have a firm base on which to work.

For almost all 'jigsaw' patterns, the most effective backsmocking stitch will be single rows of cable because this stitch is least obvious from the front and the least likely to interfere with your chosen pattern. It is worked in single rows, usually a fraction below each row of gathering to avoid catching the back-smocking in the gathering.

Backsmocking should be worked in two strands of cotton (single if using broader cotton) in the closest possible shade to the inset material, as this in no way should form a part of your pattern. It is merely a utility stitch to hold pleats in place and to give the elasticity which is so much a part of English smocking, and so comfortable to wear.

Some people choose to backsmock before starting on their chosen pattern on the front. I backsmock last, as I feel it helps to enclose all the starting and

STITCH DESCRIPTIONS

finishing necessary for 'jigsaw' patterns and generally neatens off the back. Also, I can't bear to wait another moment before starting my pattern!

You then have the opportunity to see if your work would benefit from more support, by working rows closer together. This may be necessary if your pattern on the front is fairly spaced out.

If, by any chance, after you have completed your backsmocking and removed your gathering threads, you find your pattern is still not sitting as well as you had hoped, all is not lost – it is still possible to add further rows of backsmocking to achieve the planned result!

Other backsmocking stitches, which work well but are not as well suited to this form of smocking are two- and three-step waves. It is worthwhile to work several small samplers using two-step and three-step waves to see the effects which can be achieved. Who knows, this may send you off in an entirely new direction!

Feather Stitch

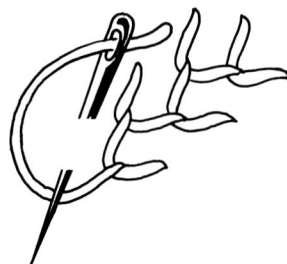

Bring the needle out at the centre top of where you wish to begin Feather Stitch. Hold the thread down with the left thumb, insert the needle a little to the right on the same level and take a small stitch down to the centre, keeping the thread under the needle point.

Insert the needle a little to the left on the same level and take another stitch to the centre, keeping the thread under the needle point.

Continue working in these two movements alternately until the required length.